BUILDING TODAY'S
GREEN HOME

BUILDING TODAY'S
GREEN HOME

PRACTICAL,
COST-EFFECTIVE AND
ECO-RESPONSIBLE
HOMEBUILDING

ART SMITH

BETTERWAY HOME
CINCINNATI, OHIO
www.popularwoodworking.com

Read This Important Safety Notice

To prevent accidents, keep safety in mind while you work. Use the safety guards installed on power equipment; they are for your protection. When working on power equipment, keep fingers away from saw blades, wear safety goggles to prevent injuries from flying wood chips and sawdust, wear hearing protection and consider installing a dust vacuum to reduce the amount of airborne sawdust in your woodshop. Don't wear loose clothing, such as neckties or shirts with loose sleeves, or jewelry, such as rings, necklaces or bracelets, when working on power equipment. Tie back long hair to prevent it from getting caught in your equipment. People who are sensitive to certain chemicals should check the chemical content of any product before using it. The authors and editors who compiled this book have tried to make the contents as accurate and correct as possible. Plans, illustrations, photographs and text have been carefully checked. All instructions, plans and projects should be carefully read, studied and understood before beginning construction. Due to the variability of local conditions, construction materials, skill levels, etc., neither the author nor Popular Woodworking Books assumes any responsibility for any accidents, injuries, damages or other losses incurred resulting from the material presented in this book. Prices listed for supplies and equipment were current at the time of publication and are subject to change.

Metric Conversion Chart

to convert	to	multiply by
Inches	Centimeters	2.54
Centimeters	Inches	0.4
Feet	Centimeters	30.5
Centimeters	Feet	0.03
Yards	Meters	0.9
Meters	Yards	1.1

Distributed in Canada by Fraser Direct
100 Armstrong Avenue
Georgetown, Ontario L7G 5S4
Canada

Distributed in the U.K. and Europe by David & Charles
Brunel House
Newton Abbot
Devon TQ12 4PU
England
Tel: (+44) 1626 323200
Fax: (+44) 1626 323319
E-mail: postmaster@davidandcharles.co.uk

Distributed in Australia by Capricorn Link
P.O. Box 704
Windsor, NSW 2756
Australia

Visit our Web site at www.popularwoodworking.com.

13   12   11   10   09   5   4   3   2   1

Library of Congress Cataloging-in-Publication Data

Smith, Art, 1948-
  Building today's green home : practical, cost-effective, and eco-responsible homebuilding / by Art Smith.
     p. cm.
  Includes bibliographical references and index.
  ISBN 978-1-55870-862-4 (pbk. : alk. paper)
  1. Ecological houses--Design and construction. 2. House construction. I. Title.

TH4860.S62 2008
690'.8047--dc22

2008022321

Acquisitions Editor: David Thiel
Senior Editor: Jim Stack
Designer: Brian Roeth
Production Coordinator: Mark Griffin
Photographer: Art Smith
Illustrators: Art Smith and Jim Stack

About the Author

Art Smith, Residential Designer, LEED AP, has had a special interest in energy-efficient yet practical homes since a crucial college decision to study engineering instead of architecture. Starting with his first passive-solar home, designed in 1980 in an Atlanta suburb, to designing current client's homes, his focus is on balancing low-energy use, low-maintenance and comfortable living — particularly for the transitioning baby-boomers. Armed with an engineering and manufacturing background,

Art, and his family, escaped the Atlanta high-tech world to the North Georgia Mountains in 2001 to continue this pursuit full-time.

Acknowledgements

To my two sweeties: Nancy & Kristina

The editors would like to thank Art, and his able-bodied photo assistant, Richard, for their above- (literally) and-beyond efforts to get just the right photos for this book.

Photo Credits:

All photos taken by the author except the following:
FIGURES 5.6, 5.7, 5.8 and 8.2: courtesy of Elk Mountain Homes
FIGURES 6.10, 6.11 and 6.12: Courtesy of EnergyEdge
FIGURES 6.23: Courtesy of Rheem Manufacturing Company
FIGURE 6.19: Courtesy of American ALDES
FIGURE 6.21: Courtesy of CONSERV
FIGURE 6.22: Courtesy of RSF Fireplaces
FIGURE 6.26: Courtesy of Infiltec Corporation
FIGURE 6.27: Courtesy of Retrotec
FIGURES 8.5, 8.6 and 8.7: Courtesy of AFM R-Control SIP
FIGURES 12.2, 12.6 and 12.9: photos by Chris Westerman

Contents

Introduction

Ever since I designed and built my first passive-solar home near Atlanta in 1980, and, more recently, clients' homes that I have designed, I have been told that I was too "far ahead". I was told that "We don't build homes *that way* around here. Curb appeal only is what sells houses." I was advised that homes had to be large to be good. Many of these suggestions were just the current trends or fads. But, what is real now? Our global warming and rising costs situation are not just passing, they are the future reality.

Building green should not be just the latest fad — it is a wise thing to do. At this phase of life of the American baby-boomers, I believe we have arrived at a crucial cross-roads. We can choose to be smart or we can choose to leave a mess for our children.

Building Today's Green Home will help you cut through the green-marketing hype and make smart choices that yield outstanding results. The eco-friendly sub categories — energy efficiency, sustainability, realistic home size, solar power and air quality — are thoroughly discussed in this book.

Using *Building Today's Green Home,* you can start your journey to either building your own home or use it as an aid in selecting a smarter and *greener* future residence.

And, my wife, Nancy, and my daughter Kristina, would like someone else to hear all this technical homebuilding jargon. They have heard this stuff for years — now it's someone else's turn!

01

The Futile Search for the Dream House

BABY-BOOMERS BEWARE! We are consuming our own retirement future as well as our children's on a futile search for the perfect dream house.

But we have time if we are smart. We can overcome this challenge with help of our typical American ingenuity coupled with the hope that the baby-boomer generation  will grasp this opportunity for greatness by choosing a simple concept — practical. Before we apply this moderating technique, how did we get to this impractical place?

Most American workers, particularly the baby boomers who are in the twilight of their careers, have felt the haunting sense that a treadmill exists in their lives. Some have felt this dread as early as their forties. The typical sequence that led to this stage is: Many went to college or trained for a better-than-average career, many worked hard for years, raised families, bought homes, cars and "stuff" and then noted that something was not fulfilling. Most of us know many examples of the midlife crisis with the afflicted person buying the sports car or motorcycle or boat that one felt was missing in the early days. I suspect that a large number of these participants will likely realize that these toys fade with a drug-like effect. In other words, the toys will need to get bigger and better to keep the treadmill of satisfaction going. I believe that the American pursuit of the dream house is a crucial model of this behavior. The current mortgage industry "sub-prime" crisis is just one validating sample of the social price of this excess behavior.

A particularly American characteristic provides a key clue to the source: Fads. Americans not only like fads, we embrace them, even if subconsciously. Some examples outside the housing industry demonstrate the same pattern evident in specific housing samples discussed later. One of the best fad areas is our second most expensive life purchase: automobiles. Chapters could be written on just the range of American tastes for each decade. A few specific examples, principally focused on the cosmetics of cars are a good test of this theory.

Have you even noticed while watching a movie, say, ten to twenty years old, how dated the cars look, particularly American models? Focus on the cars that had vinyl roofs. Most would think that these vinyl tops now look silly. Guess what, they were silly then! We were cloaked in the emperor's-new-clothes mentality of what was in fashion. As a test of this concept, I'll provide several car models of different decades.

1940's: 1940 Ford
1950's: Jaguar XKE, Porsche 356
1960's: 1964 Ford Mustang, 1969-72
        Datsun 240Z
1970's: 1976 Volkswagen Scirroco
1980's: 1986-89 Acura Integra, 1987
        Honda Civic-S
1990's: 1990 Honda Civic-S, 1989-93
        Nissan Maxima

Take an automotive-history stroll via your chosen Internet search engine of these examples and two distinct trends will appear. First, they will likely not have vinyl roofs and in general, they will still appear to be attractive despite the car's age. The essential discovery is that these particular car models are designed with a clean shape and not over-loaded with excessive design trim such as abundant chrome, exaggerated body details, etc. As a counter to this concept look at some of the excess of fins on the late 1950's American Cars. (Yes, I know some are classics to some serious collectors, 1956 and 1957 Chevys, etc.) Most of us have at least one story of a college friend or acquaintance that unfortunately had to claim the ownership of a Gremlin or Pacer or some other exotic styling experiment. Also, everyone will have their own favorite cars other than the above example list. My point is that beyond each of our emotional attachment to specific cars of our eras, there is a general trend that the ones that appear to improve in time did not have styling excesses.

Another related automotive trending concept is the added optional appearance packages. Take a close look, particularly on some of the mid-size to larger SUV models, at the extra two-tone color enhancements around the rocker panels and fender openings. Do you remember the simulated-wood (plastic) side panels of the mid-to-late 1980's minivans? The automotive marketing wiz's were apparently trying to appeal to the 1960's flashback visions of the Woody wagon at the California surfing beach. What happened in the modern version is that they utilized cheap-looking plastic to attempt to simulate the real wood of the older product. (Pause and ponder this concept momentarily. This effect will occur in the housing industry examples shown later.) Some of the color and trim shapes will be fun to look at in future movie. Yes, the same syndrome of the "old-movie cars" will be déjà vu.

An even more subtle before-and-after comparison, taken from the above automobile list, will show another twist to this point of excesses. The 1984 Honda Civic-S originally came with a grey two-tone lower body color below the mid-door body side molding line. (I suspect that the Japanese designers were trying to "Americanize" the Civic-S.) Thus, a red 1984-1986 Civic S had this additional wide gray lower section. About 1987, Honda changed the S so the lower panel color matched the main body color. Check your Internet searches again to see which held the more attractive appearance over time. Yes, the cleaner, simpler 1987 model wins again. (By the way, I consciously painted my own red 1986 Honda S red, over the gray two-tone lower panel before Honda made this change in production models.)

1964 Ford Mustang

stand up in time and ironically looked much worse with aging. Thus, we added fodder to the American throw-away mentality!

In the American housing industry, one sees a similar "fad" pattern. A test of this trend can be found in almost any near-city neighborhood that is significantly older than the newer exploding suburbs. This near-city scenario is particularly evident if the neighborhood has had gaps in development or has multiple cycles of re-development. If that neighborhood had vacant-lot gaps that were built on later, you can almost always see the building trends of that era frozen on that former vacant lot. Also, as neighborhoods go through their second and third re-births, you likely see the current popular architectural style (or fad) blended into the additions and major renovations of the original style. (More on this renovation issue relating to infill "McMansions" later in Chapter 6.) Thus, as one travels through these types of neighborhoods, you can visually grasp the passing of these styles/fads. Note: The extreme styles will fade, as do fashions.

My current favorite example of American housing fad's is a validation of the entire point of this chapter — the Arts-&-Crafts style. As a residential designer on many unique building locations and a range of client's tastes, I'm amazed at how many times that I have heard Arts-&-Crafts or Bungalow/Craftsman style used. I have heard it used in weekend mountain chalets (or cabin), traditional suburban developments and even in log homes. But what I see implemented is the same pattern of extremes or excesses. As architecture historians will attest, Arts-&-Crafts was a revolt against the excessively-decorated Victorian homes. Quite simply, not many clients could afford to build or even maintain the lavish homes of that era. The original Arts-&-Crafts, even the true Craftsman homes, were significantly more practical (that practical word again), less ornamented and reasonably-sized than the preceding Victorians.

Frank Lloyd Wright's Prairie Style generally followed this focus on function rather than ornamentation for decorating purposes.

As a personal test to this excess trim syndrome, I had the unfortunate opportunity to talk to a local long-term automobile body shop owner. We had a late night meeting with a small bear cub in the Georgia mountain road returning from a trip to visit my daughter at her college campus. The minor body damage still required a few day's stay in the shop. While waiting in the lobby, I noticed an early 1990's Nissan Maxima SE from the above "clean car" example list. I engaged the shop owner about how the Maxima was still attractive despite its fifteen-year age. He confirmed that same opinion. I then brought up the vinyl roof issue to ask about his experiences of seeing many of these vehicles over the years. He almost rolled his eyes and mentioned something about those "Landau roofs". A dissertation by him on the difficulty of repairing them and other excessive automotive trim follies pursued. I wasn't the only one who noticed this fad.

I also noticed this excess trim in the industrial design of other products. Early in my career, I worked with small high-tech start-up firms. My responsibilities grew from designing and later managing the "industrial design" look of an electronic product. I frequently found excessive marketing pressure on the designers and the designer's own desires to make the product "look good" at all costs. No one desires an unattractive product, of course, but this pressure frequently resulted in products that looked flashy, but were difficult to manufacture, and frequently had quality issues with these cosmetic compromises. And, just like in the automotive industry, these cosmetic add-ons did not

Some specific exaggerations of the current version of Arts-&-Crafts are in the areas of trim and colors. Most of the classic Bungalows of the early 1900s in America typically had one color of trim, maybe a second. The current color trend is multiple colors, typically three to four. The range of textures used has increased from one or two or more (shingle, board-and-batten, lap siding, stone and brick) in the same house elevation. Also, the over-use of elaborate crown molding, I believe, was more typical of Victorians than the true Arts-&-Crafts homes. This trim exaggeration reminds me of the famous story of the young talented architect, Howard Roark, in Ayn Rand's *The Fountainhead*. Howard was resisting the architecture dean's push for his class project to include classic, but ornate Corinthian-style columns. Howard's insistence on his own design being very clean rather than the typical ornate designs of his classmates, thus choosing function over form, led to his dismissal from architecture school. (Later in his novel life he wins with this function-over-form strategy, as did Frank Lloyd Wright.)

My personal Howard Roark pet-peeve example is roof dormers used to excess. I have seen many houses, even single-story designs (ranches), that have fake dormers. Yes, you can actually see the rafters of the roof through the window. It is not used as a dormer for its normal functional purpose, but is simply added for look. Note also that the steeper roof pitch associated with the dormer-roof styling is also a related topic (covered in detail in Chapter 5). I have seen many multiple dormers placed so closely together that I can't imagine how the siding contractor was able to nail siding in the gaps between them. Note that by utilizing three small dormers, if intended for the typical reason of increasing space in the second floor, is then negated by multiple small zones

1940 Ford Coupe

too small for use. A future hint to ponder: What does a dormer actually add to the cost of construction of the home? (More later.) Another teaser — think about how you would add gutters to different dormer's design types. Where do the drain pipes go and what is their impact? Again, the draw of the fad is simply to gain "look".

My second-best example is increasingly complex roofs. American suburban subdivision roof designs have become so elaborate that I think I have discovered the unwritten "six-foot" rule. That is, one cannot have a home in the neighborhood unless the maximum length of any roof segment is six feet. In other words, within six feet, a roof section has to make a change in direction or shape, thus netting a more elaborate-looking roof design. A specific example is the use of double-gable rakes on one side of a protruding gable. Adding to this excess is the return cornice trim that is added to both the single rake and the double rake on one side. Looking at the cost of these extra trim features, and the more complex framing details, to a typical project and comparing their cost to improving the quality of the other related materials is a fundamental exercise covered in detail later. However, by just comparing these extra-trim concepts in a house to the above automobile example is intriguing. Relating these two different industries confirms to me the strong pull of American fads.

In John Naisbitt's 1982 book *Megatrends*, he made a clear distinction between fads and true megatrends. One particular megatrend is eerily related to our own future home choices on two levels. This trend, *high-tech, soft-touch*, outlines the concept that as we become more high-tech in the fast-changing information age, we need more soft things to balance out our life — nature, woods, lakes, mountains, less-crowded environments, etc. This first level of soft-touch relates to the physical location of a new home. Most American families have shared family vacations

1955 Jaguar

to mountain cabins, lakes or even the old-time small beach towns. As we age, I believe the lure of this slower pace increases as we move farther into our hectic and busy careers coupled with the general complexity of the family tasks. Does one feel as relaxed at a modern crowded beach town with concrete high-rise condominiums or the little beach cabin? Why do we see the freeways crowded with all the hastily exiting cars from the Atlanta, Georgia metro areas on Friday afternoons, aiming for the North Georgia Appalachians? Soft-touch! Same for Lake Tahoe in California, The Berkshires in Massachusetts, the White Mountains in New Hampshire, The Rockies in Colorado, and on and on — soft-touch.

I reflect on the numerous times that our family headed to our Georgia mountain cabin and the sighs of relief that filled us as we stepped out on the deck to enjoy our Appalachian landscape. It was the perfect antidote to the Atlanta high-tech rush. This resulting growth for second homes in America during the late 1980s and into the 1990s, especially in mountain sites, small towns and beaches, validates Mr. Naisbitt's premise of soft-touch in the location phase.

Another significant trend related to soft-touch is revealed by reviewing the American population centers from the early 1900s into the early 2000s. Most small towns, particularly away from major cities, either lost population or at best stayed even in the 1900s. The years of going to my high-school reunions in a small western Alabama town confirmed this pattern. In fact, some of my classmates who stayed in the small town, noted that the local population decreased. However, small American towns, even as far as 40-80 miles out from an Atlanta, Georgia size metropolitan area began growing at a significant rate around the early 1990s. This growth was not the usual suburban sprawl. One key segment of the homes built then were second homes by middle-to-prosperous baby-boomers. Note also that this time period was when the leading edge of the baby-boomer wave was approaching mid careers and likely phasing out of the child-rearing years. A good microcosm of this population is in our own North Georgia community, specifically, observing the changes in our Board of Directors. In the early 1990s, years after we owned our future building lot, but prior to building, the vast majority

of the twelve-member board were of retiring age (pre-baby-boomers, greatest generation era). Some lived full-time in the community, but many were still weekenders at this more than 20-year-old development. Moving into the late 1990s and early 2000, the faces changed. More and more baby-boomers were represented in this body of people. This was not just a normal age shift, but a cultural shift as depicted in *Megatrends*. Some folks had given up careers in the Atlanta area, downsized and were living full-time in "the mountains". Some were still in their late forties to mid-fifties. A growth in children waiting for the school bus increased even though there was not a significant growth in the percentage of child-rearing age parents. Most were baby-boomers that still had older children or, like our family, had a child later in life (also somewhat of a baby-boomer trend). In other words, they were not retired yet but they were already downsizing.

My observations in the booming Atlanta area were similar to numerous other regions visited over years of business trips and relative's contacts. For example, in New England, the population growth of New Hampshire's, Vermont's and Maine's small towns located away from central Boston is well-documented. Beyond this specific Boston-based push to escape the areas' tax burden is another soft-touch effect. A significant portion of this population is not just searching for a reasonably-priced principal home coupled with the reality of longer commutes. Many of these new homes are either second homes, weekenders or retirement homes. Two of my New England relatives made transitions out of the Boston area with their decisions similar to the soft-touch effect. Interesting to note: I have had many discussions with both sisters for years, prior to these transitions, on the last-home concept mingled with shades of us desiring to get away from the rat race. One sister, Penny, lived in the greater Boston area for many years in Waltham, which is, coincidently, near the famous Route 128 high-tech corridor. As she approached retirement, Penny chose to sell her family home in Waltham and move out from the Boston area. She selected a quaint and lovely town — Greenfield, Massachusetts. A mere 99 miles west of Boston. In our discussions, Penny never used the phrase soft-touch, but her motives fit the pattern.

My other sister, Sandy, went through a similar change. Sandy and her husband had an active business life in the closer-in Boston area of Malden. For years they had vacationed in the New Hampshire Mountain/Lake areas, staying in a cabin or two. Before approaching retirement age, in the eastern edge of New Hampshire, near rural Maine, they built a lake-front home that was more than a week-end cabin. What was this new cabin's distance from Boston? Over 100 miles, more than a commuting distance, it was an escape distance. Sandy and I had discussed the rat-race-get-away home idea before my family spent a weekend with them at their new lake home. This lakeside cabin was like a retire-ment home, but retirement was still several years away. As we were making our own downsizing life transition out of the hectic Atlanta Suburbs to a small North Georgia mountain town named Ellijay, Sandy planned to continue their primary business lives in Boston and utilize the lake house as a week-ender. Over the next couple of years we noted the lure to the lake pulling on Sandy's plans. Sandy and her husband changed their business situation and moved to the New Hampshire lake house much earlier than planned. Soft-touch can be strong!

Another friend's example of this shift occurred in two phases during his retirement years. Hunter had been a business associate for almost thirty years in the Atlanta high-tech industry. As the owner of a manufacturer's rep firm, he called on my business, showing us products that we could design into our end product. Over the years we had frequent networking lunches where we cov-ered many topics, including life transitional issues. Around the late 1990s, when our family was plan-ning to downsize and move from Atlanta to our mountain cabin, Hunter was selling his long-term Atlanta home and property. He was engaged in searching for a retirement-home setting. He first considered a small South Georgia com-munity (slower pace, lower home costs, etc.). However, he chose an upscale North Georgia mountain-style develop-ment that had a small-town feel. Even though he had downsized from his suburban home, his new home was still

about 2,800 square feet. During the next five years, his upscale mountain community had surged in growth (the Atlanta get-away crowd was fueling this frenzy). His new mountain community grew from a small town to a city in just five years. The trend that led him to the mountains killed the original reason. He downsized again. He moved back closer to Atlanta to a newer community with floor plans and an environment targeted at retir-ees. Retirement tax-credit issues and family needs were also factored in this change. I told Hunter that if we had videotaped our two lunch meetings at the beginning and end of these five years, he would be amused at the transition in attitudes and awareness. Both times I was consistent in talking about the downsizing rat-race syndrome and how it would affect our home choices. Hunter wanted to live in a smaller house with a simpler lifestyle and he did it — twice!

I observed another level to the soft-touch trend in the architectural style choices clients were mak-ing. An example of this is watching a person perus-ing the homebuilding magazine racks. The draw of the warm interior of the log home or timber-frame style captures their attention. My hunch is that the person is looking for or dreaming of an escape from today's high-tech pressure The warmth of the natural wood asserts a strong pull. Going beyond this initial wood-color trigger is the floor plan. This person desires a simpler floor plan with an "open" concept. Most designers and realtors confirm this by noting that the traditional dining room is disap-pearing. I believe it is a basic desire to have less furniture, clutter and complexity as this phase of life approaches. Thus, materialistic downsizing is a soft-touch. Warm wood, when carried to extremes, has its burdens. See Chapter 10.

Americans have been known throughout history to think big — a Texas-size sort of thing. For example, most early baby-boomers spent their younger years in a typical American ranch home of about 1,000 square feet. The average home is now about 2,000 square feet. I challenge the concept that big is better, particularly in one's home. This thought becomes

1986 Honda Acura Integra

evident after a baby-boomer family has lived in a few homes through the progression of increased home needs and values. As the family size grows and career

1970-1973 Datsun 240Z

advancements occur, the house (and the accompanying furniture and "stuff") follows suit. I suspect, after a few levels of growth, that most people begin to sense that larger size and more stuff has its burden. For example, one trend in American suburban homes has been to have huge, entry foyers. I feel what I call the "elevator shaft" effect in large foyers or cathedral ceilings in living rooms (or great rooms). The tall ceiling does not feel comfortable or cozy to many people. Once one gets beyond the initial "wow effect" of this huge space, an uncomfortable "hugeness" seems to be in place. Sarah Susanka's first book, *Not So Big House, The: A Blueprint for the Way We Really Live,* published in 1998, addressed this uniquely American fad. In fact, I believe Sarah's choice of the title, *Not so Big,* was made because she realized that most Americans reacted negatively to *small*. She said that we were building big homes, not ones with character. My own experience with residential projects confirms this.

One version of a big-is-not-cozy scenario was shown on a recent airing of *This Old House*. The host was visiting the Wickwires, fifteen years after the show's project of constructing this most famous timber-frame, barn-like home. In fact, the scene of this timber-frame erection was in the background of the opening and closing moments of the show for years. As the new host entered the majestic two-story, New England barn-sized foyer, he raved about the beautiful and impressive tall timber-frame workmanship. He noted that this must surely be the Wickwires' favorite spot in the house. With my simplistic paraphrasing of their response, their answer was their favorite spot was actually a cozy, low-ceilinged nook in the rear of the house. I have been in many huge and majestic traditional timber-frame homes and I've noticed that the beautiful, hand-crafted woodwork is physically far away (thus appearing smaller) and seems colder.

One of my favorite residential design techniques that I have used over the years demonstrates the reverse of this "big" approach — the window seat. This concept has appeared in recent articles as a good design concept to utilize in smaller homes. In our North Atlanta suburban home (1981-2001), I used a window seat between two closets flanking a window zone in the master bedroom. I fondly remember my daughter coming up to this spot many times as a toddler. She would jump up and nestle among the pillows. She had her "little spot". This cozy nook had some nurturing affect. Many years later, in our Walnut Mountain EnergyStar model home project (see Chapter 12), I used a window seat in the second bedroom, not the master bedroom. A key component of this nook design is spacing timber trusses in the seat zone coupled with the ceiling tongue-and-groove pine decking. These strategic wood-based features contribute to this nook's warmth. My daughter, now college age, also loved this second-bedroom design in the new EnergyStar house. The bedroom still had a reasonably-sized cathedral ceiling for spaciousness (ranging from 8' at the eave/seat area to about 13' at the peak). The window seat is the prominent detail. This cozy-sized nook, which was not huge, drew one in.

Another facet of this "big" syndrome is how many acquaintances have moved to new, larger homes and then later noticed the vast amount of furniture (stuff) needed to fill the space. Obviously, one might not fill the large rooms with furniture overnight, simply because of the time and effort required of this task. I have witnessed many rooms in these "starter castles" without furniture for years. I have even seen a traditional dining room filled with an assortment of toddler's toys because the owner simply had too many rooms to fill with furniture. Thus, a mini-McMansion playroom was born! In America, most people have the ability, and the right, to make these lifestyle choices. My observation is that home choices made during the larger-space-needed era of rearing a family and later preparing for retirement period *are vastly different*.

Yet, the big-is-better fad's influence is out of balance during this later phase of life when the kids are gone.

Another trend is the focus on two-story homes in current developments. I frequently see what appears to be an aversion to anything that resembles a ranch-style home. Couple this with some subdivisions that have an architectural requirement that the roof pitch must be steeper than 9/12 (required to be bigger but not better). I have noted this pattern in clients from Florida who are planning a second home in mountainous regions like Georgia, North Carolina, etc. I suspect that two major factors are in play here. The first may likely be a desire for change in appearance from the 1950' and 1960's ranch homes that many American baby-boomers considered childhood homes. Also, due to the Florida hurricane-resistance issue, lower peaked, frequently hipped, not end-gabled roofs are the norm. The look of lower-profile homes is the typical appearance in their neighborhoods up to this life stage. Second, the steep-pitched and wood sided mountain chalet look has the emotional draw of simply being "a cabin". Ask the question of this two-story house design: Do you want to frequently climb stairs in this phase of your life? Thus, the emotional side can have more pull than the rational side in home choices.

One example of big that demonstrates the lack of usefulness is seen in mountain and/or lake side cabins with decks. Since a sloping lot is frequently a factor in vacation/weekender or getaway homes due to geography (unless you are in Kansas or Oklahoma), there is usually a basement. In extreme mountain settings, a sub-wall situation can exist. This means that there is a structural wall, hopefully conservatively made using reinforced poured concrete below the basement level.

We frequently see from a few feet to as much as twelve feet of sub-wall. As the buildable mountain building lots fill up and more extreme lots become the last choice on which to build, there can be 13' to 20' under the deck location to the ground at the house wall. At the end of the deck, the supporting posts can be several more feet high. These cabins are a chalet style, implying a loft or at least a partial second floor. I have seen decks added to all three levels. On first glance it seems to fit the zone. However, due to the size and materials needed, I rarely see superior material used or good bracing techniques. The project size chosen is so huge that the client cannot afford to pay for higher-quality materials or a safer design. The sad things is that, after driving by many of these multiple decks when the owners are present, I rarely see anyone using the extra decks. They usually use the most convenient one — off of the kitchen or dining room. In Chapter 3, we will compare costs and techniques to gain some understanding that using sustainable materials doesn't cost much over the long run. Several major deck failures in the Atlanta metro area over the years have been publicized. Many of these were large decks which resulted in injuries. What is the real cost of this sad situation? "Big" is a key element of the problem!

Why does this big effect have anything to do with future life and home choices? I believe that Americans spend more time and money chasing after extra stuff, which contributes to the rat-race treadmill. We spend a lot of time crowding the malls on the weekends buying stuff. Then we get up early on Monday to go work to go pay for the stuff we just bought to fill up the huge spaces. Surveys have shown that the American work week continues to increase in length (working harder than ever). We may have even passed the industrious Japanese in working longer hours! There are likely other factors, but I attest that the bigger-home, more-stuff chase is a major contributor.

Another facet of big houses is related to energy costs. Future energy costs are likely to climb at a growth rate much worse than we plan for. The cost of energy needed to maintain the comfort level in these large zones is large. (See Chapter 6.) The emotional reasons for choosing the look of steep roofs (sometimes stated as "adds architectural interest") needs to be addressed. Also there's a technical issue. Here are two stories about comfort concerns.

A family friend is now in retirement and had downsized from a medium-large, two-story home with a basement. She was still in the Atlanta metro area. They moved to a ranch-style home with a basement that was reasonably-sized (about 2,400 square feet). One day, our conversation moved to monthly energy costs. She said that the new, smaller home still had monthly utility bills over $200 per month. Her final comment went something like this: "But we keep the thermostat at 62° in the winter and 78° in the summer." I know my current, smaller passive-solar home (second version) is too radical for most suburban architectural tastes, has likely never been below 62°. Typically, on a cold night the house will lower to 67-68° and warm back up to the low 70s by the end of a sunny (and cold) winter day with minor heat pump assistance. The question for us to ponder about these two homes is one's comfort. As we head into retirement is all of this "fashion" worth it?

Another conversation with another friend about their energy costs and comfort shows how the cost of energy and size interplay. This couple bought a larger (about 3,000 square foot, two-story) home in a newer upscale subdivision. They are in their early to mid-fifties and their only child has long left the home nest. Their earlier home was smaller, with a finished basement and I believe the mortgage was completely paid. Their discussions related to a video interview that I emailed to them about our EnergyStar model home (Chapter 12) done by ChoosingGreen.com. The video tour emphasized specific construction details that we incorporated in this project to achieve low power consumption while using a total electric concept combined with a low-maintenance exterior. We stressed that many of the features were hidden and not easy for the consumer to see or know of their existence or importance. As my friends and I talked, they expressed concern about their new home's energy costs, which, combining the electric and gas, were about $350 to $400 per month. The concluding response was: "But we mainly huddle up only in the master bedroom". Is this a comfortable existence? I don't get it.

The technical side of comfort relative to the size and shape of houses is that it's difficult to control

the temperature in a tall house with a two-story foyer. The normal stratification of air is basic thermodynamics: heat rises. I know that you can have huge fans, even "turbo props" cycling the air furiously. But for what? Running all the time? What happens when the power is off? I know friends here in this hotbed of mountain retirement communities where their steep, 12/12 pitched mountain-chalet roofs have a loft with this problem. The cosmetic lure of the loft is easily outweighed by the reality that in the summer months, the increased heat up there is not worth occupying the space — even with a fan continuously trying to win the thermodynamic battle. Even well-insulated homes, like the EnergyStar model home, will have this effect, but it is lessened.

The interesting paradox to this loft effect is similar to the cozy feel of the window seat. The comfort price is the penalty of this choice. Most homes with lofts are usually poorly insulated. They exhibit a double-whammy in the wrong direction since these tall-style homes will not be comfortable (in temperature) without a power-robbing solution.

What is the problem with these curb appeal cosmetic factors? The most expensive item that we will purchase in our lifetime, our home, has both the perception and reality of being a poor product! A January 2004 article in *Consumer Reports* aptly bore the title *Housewrecked*. One expert noted that with about one million new homes built annually in America, 15% have serious problems. That's about 150,000 homes with serious-level defects actually identified. How many more had medium or small problems lurking? A quote from the executive of the respected Boston-area consulting firm, Building Sciences Corp., beautifully linked the cosmetic and quality issues: "People are willing to pay for Jacuzzis and marble counters, when they should be concerned about the quality of the house". My experience with residential clients is consistent with the above quotation. Note that the residential construction building code, however mature and solid with testing over the years is simply "the minimum". That is, it is not "good practice" or even "better practice". Thus, when one actually determines that a problem exists in your expensive purchase, many years may have passed, with the cumulative costs not recoverable. A paraphrasing of a quotation in a Steve McQueen movie helps emphasis this time-

1976 Volkswagen Scirocco

delay effect. Steve's character, in the 1960's era "The Magnificent Seven" was relating their assessment of the difficult situation in their story. He said that this reminded him of someone falling off of a twenty story building. As he fell past each floor, he commented: "Nineteenth floor, everything's okay so far, eighteenth floor, everything's okay so far...". Time is like gravity — you can't go back. We need to *think* more about the many decisions in our future retirement homes, not just *feel* about the cosmetics that anyone can spot in the curb-appeal from the street. My goal is to provide information to help you in this journey of discovery.

First however, I want to provide some monetary examples, with expansion on their source in the following related technical sections to help you, the reader, sense the impact of time and cost as mentioned above. These monthly estimates, are just that, estimates, particular to our Southeast Region of the United States. Regional styles, geography, labor costs and specific exterior finishes impact these dollar amounts. However, I believe that these North Georgia based figures are roughly typical for most of America. Our North Georgia area is in Climate Zone 4 of the International Building Code, 2006. This means that our climate is similar to a large portion of many middle-America states. We also have a reasonably long summer with many very hot days, not significantly different from Atlanta. We also have colder, and slightly longer winters than Atlanta. Using technical sources, you will find that our region shows up as a good, mid-level test point. Being in the Appalachian Mountain region, we can have windy periods as well as significant rainy times. All these factors contribute to the energy costs as well as exterior maintenance and structure issues of the region's homes.

Before we define these costs, my version of a well-known 1992 election slogan comes to mind: "It's not just the original cost, energy costs, maintenance costs, and tax creep dummy, it is all of them."

Original cost means the price that one paid for an object at the time of purchase, or in the case of a home, not just the entire completed home, but a specific feature that one chose for the home, for example, brick exterior vs. wood exterior. For original cost, I will assume that one still has a mortgage and will be using a 30-year mortgage at a 6% inter-est rate. Later, some of these concepts will build on the fact many baby-boomers will hopefully have enough equity in their larger home to not have a mortgage during retirement for their downsized version. But, some statistics and market issues indicate a mortgage in retirement may still be a reality for many and this fact will enhance the importance of strategies discussed later. It is important to remember that the original cost of an object is *not the complete cost*. This is missed most of the time or simply glossed over in the emotion of the home purchase or planning. For example, the real cost of a simple wood-sided exterior is not just the material cost, the labor cost and the stain finish. It is linked to the maintenance costs more than most understand. A dollar example from one of our mountain chalet projects bears this out. A 1,450 square foot chalet had a $5,000 original cost in material and labor for the lapped wood-siding exterior. The original budget for the exterior stain job was about $2,600. In just three years, a new staining was required at a cost of $5,000, with evidence that it was actually needed much earlier. Even with this better-quality second staining, the fear is that this expensive exercise will approach sooner than one realizes. Using 36 months, the maintenance costs linked to the wood exterior is averaging about $140 per month. As a sanity check, I discussed these costs with a well-respected local painting contractor and his estimate to clients was to plan for about $100 per month or more for maintenance costs for wood-sided cabins. Another factor is that some of the wood had been already replaced and more should have been replaced. This made the repair project costs even higher. The third element of true cost is exposed: Replacement costs. The real cost for a construction feature is original costs, maintenance costs and the eventual and dreaded replacement costs. They are linked even if you don't want them to be.

A retired friend's experience with rising costs for the replacement factor bears telling. This family, retired for years, had lived near to us for most of my daughter's childhood in an Atlanta suburb. They sold their house and moved to a nearby single-level retirement-styled house for several years. Then they moved to our new mountain town, about 75 miles north. This last- home choice was a 2,000 square foot ranch, with ten years of aging. Not long after he moved to the mountain community, we were building one of my Timber-Truss, Energy-Efficient, SIP construction (Structural Insulated Panel) Ranch-style designs nearby. (Well, almost a ranch. It had a small loft and basement — about 1400 square feet of main-living space). The builder agreed to my recommendation of a good-quality aluminum-clad exterior window, EnergyStar rated (with low-maintenance exterior and low-energy use goals in mind). We chose casement-and-awning vs. builder-priced double-hung wood style. My retired friend was having difficulty heating his new/old home during the winter months with a heat pump. After much exploring and testing, they finally determined the principal culprit was the lower-grade windows and a poor-quality installation of them. There were leaks and gaps all around the windows that were, of course, not evident, nor were known, during the realtor's proud tour of the home to the eventual owners, my friends. My friend then had most of the windows replaced and installed properly at about the same period we were installing the windows in the nearby new project, and the costs were about the same — around $8,000. For a more accurate comparison: His larger home had more windows and the quality of his new windows were markedly improved over the originals, but not of the same quality as the windows of the new Timber Home. (It would have cost about $24 per month extra to have had this quality of windows installed during the original construction. Rather than the one-time, big-bang dollar figure years later while in retirement.)

For a typical weekend cabin, let's use a maintenance figure of $150-$200 per month over a fifteen-to-twenty year baby-boomer expected retirement. I will choose $200 per month because my experience shows surprises will occur and inflation will average this figure upward. Note that one of these little surprises could be a substantial item, like replacing all of the wood siding.

Energy costs for the above cabin, with typical construction and a mix of gas heating and electric cooling is around $200 per month. Since we have a regional mix of a large, cost-effective power utility and a more costly local EMC electric utility, I believe that this figure is close. Going to the extremes of analysis-paralysis should also take into account of the time effect of inflation. I have a good thirty-five-year gauge of electric kilowatt-per- hour

costs in one of the better-served power localities and this figure seems to average the trend well. (By the way, the above "new" Timber home near my friend's window-replacement home, when we last checked with the owners, the monthly energy bills were averaging about $75 combined gas and electric costs. Yes, the house with the "expensive" windows.)

This conserving energy idea is not limited to a minority. The September 2007 issue of *Tec Home Magazine* cited a survey from the Consumer Electronics Association regarding future homes. The number one issue involved energy-efficiency of their next home. What was significant, as reported by the Shelton Group, was that 78% of the time during the home-buying process, *no one talked to them about the energy topic!* Not the realtor, not the contractor, not the banker and so on. What a disconnect!

Now let's estimate Tax Creep. It occurs in growth areas. If one checks into the history of the 1979 Proposition 13 in California, the extent of this burden is known. Since California is a key Bell-Weather state, as noted by the book *MegaTrends*, it makes sense that tax creep would occur there. Proposition 13, simply addressed, was a taxpayer's revolt against the local tax assessors raising property taxes too quickly. Our own family-tax experiences should provide a relative example due to the somewhat Bell-Weather effect of our two different home locales. First, our own 1980's suburban Atlanta home (with passive solar) was around 1,920 square feet of heated space plus a two-car garage. Our home's significance was that it was located in Gwinnett County, Georgia. Gwinnett is a poster-child for American "suburbanization". For example, Gwinnett frequently appeared in census surveys during the early-to-late 1980s as one of the fastest growing counties in the U.S. A rough population summary will hit one in the head of this magnitude of growth. In 1980, Gwinnett had about 180,000 people in a fairly large physical land area located northeast of Atlanta, about fifteen miles at the closest point to downtown Atlanta. By 2007, the county population was over 750,000. Little ole Georgia has had a California type syndrome! But what of the property taxes for our home? In 1980 they were about $1,000 annually. Our last full year, 2000, the county only taxes had grown to $2,500 annually (there was a small city tax also). As a reference, our current intentionally-small cabin (passive solar, energy efficient, low-maintenance exterior, etc.) has 1,250 sq. ft. for the main floor plus a half basement had a tax bill of about $700 in 1998. We are now $1,100 annually in a rural, but growing mountain community (Those darn trends again.) I expect that some New Englanders, New Yorkers and even some Californians will feel that we "have it good" compared to their burdens. Nevertheless, the specific numbers will be relative for your zones, but will still bear out the pattern. So let's compromise and say that the property taxes will average only $150 dollars a month.

Before I summarize all of these costs, a tax-creep story of an acquaintance comes to mind that points to these tax costs and also to a strategy we will develop later. This acquaintance, a retired, single lady was just completing a new home in a nice upscale community. This new home was a ranch style, about 2,100 square feet on one level, plus a matching basement. It had a one car garage. She was moving from a difficult living site, high on a mountain with a Chalet-style (two floors), wood-sided cabin. (Yes, maintenance costs, etc. were also factors in this move.) At a social function, as we were discussing her new home, she posed a question to me that sparked a twist to her question that she had not considered. Her question regarded the technical permit issues about completely finishing her basement. My first response was a question back to her asking her if she had considered the impact on her property taxes by completing the entire basement's 2,100 square feet? Even though this space would be typically valued by an appraiser at a lower rate than the main floor, it would still be a substantial boost in the home's appraisal. Thus, her house assessment approaches that of a 4,000 square foot house! I'm not sure, but my estimate is that her taxes will be close to $300 per month. The key here is the starting point of her tax costs will be at this new higher level, not the earlier home's cost. Just another point of reference!

So a quick dollar-per-month summary for these few cost items is now apparent. Let's say that these three key items are $550 per month. Average this monthly figure without the time value of inflation and interest (Some CPA's can do this detail analysis on their own if they want), and using a 20-year baby-boomer expected retirement period and presto, we have over $130,000 in fixed costs over their mortgage. Guess what — most of us will not be that lucky to have only these costs. My experience with many baby-boomers in their current homes may even double this figure. Some surveys on baby-boomer retirement savings indicate only about 25% of us have more than $100,000 saved for retirement. Most of their assets are the equity in their homes! So we can eat up a lot of our monetary future and our children's if we are not smart.

Another way to understand this monetary impact globally is to look at the baby-boomer group. The assumed number for this American segment totals about 76 million, born from 1946 to 1964. One gauge of this number is to think in these terms: Every day in America, more than 10,000 turn 60 years of age, 55 years and 50.

What a wave coming — a veritable human tsunami in transition. Even if you accept one estimate that only 20% of this group will downsize and assume 67% home ownership and do a rough yearly average, potentially 300 thousand homes per year will be needed for this market. Compare this one special segment to the total U.S. annual new-home market ranging from 1 million to 1.2 million over the last several years. I believe it to be as significant an issue as the forecasted baby-boomer hit on Social Security! These two issues are profoundly interrelated.

Before we start to work a solution toward sanity, a popular description of insanity, attributed to Albert Einstein comes to mind: "Doing the same thing over and over, and expecting a different result". Thus, like the known principal in the computer age of "Garbage in, garbage out", we have to do something different to get different results! The typical construction industry solution on how not to improve is: "Putting a Band-Aid on a broken leg". We will need much more than a Band-Aid for this problem.

> Every day in America, more than 10,000 people (baby-boomers) turn 60, 55 and 50 years of age.

The momentum resisting change is almost insurmountable, so this effort to change must also be of major proportions. I'll outline two points about how difficult it is to change and later relate strategies to overcome this force. First, I see the residential-building industry working mainly via two main processes. (I will later suggest a third, particularly for our baby-boomer market.) Most homes are built as *spec*, meaning *speculation* (similar to being in the roller coaster of the stock market). It doesn't matter if this is a huge, successful builder with tract homes, or the small town builder whose family has been building one or two annually for generations. Their general operational mode is the same, they build to whatever their formula has evolved to and hope that prospective buyers, with some minor customizations, will chose their end product. Note that they are still guessing about the hot trend, colors, floor plan style, size, etc. Thus, the *risk* factor in spec building. However, what they build is generally dictated by the draw spread sheets from banks. One example that has been in a typical bank sheet for many years, without updating even with the building code realities, is a comparison of two line items. The line item budget for insulation is about 1%. Thus, for around $200,000 for the cost of your house, your insulation budget is only $2000. If you understand even the more current updates to the Energy Codes of the International Building Code (which is the minimum) and the different-quality insulating technologies, a truly well-built home will easily exceed this insulation budget limitation. As a reference point, we spent close to $10,000 in insulation techniques in the EnergyStar Model home, including solid-foam R31 panels in the roof (cathedral, non-vented roof style) and spray-foam R19 in the 2×6 walls.

The draw sheet line item for interior trim, is 4% for interior trim, thus an $8,000 budget here. You will see the same pattern for the critical window budget. The effort required for a builder, even a larger, more established firm, to overcome and finance the differences of this budgeting pattern to build a better quality product is tremendous. For the small town builder, like my builder friend Richard (Band-Aid quote source) who desires to improve his product, this challenge is like climbing Mount Everest. I can relate many experiences of simply convincing clients/builders to use 2×6 framing over 2×4s as trying. This slight increase in cost, in the range of $300-$600, is difficult to obtain. By the way, at one point in just the last couple of years, 2×4-8' studs were only $.25 less than 2×6-8' studs. Thus, to "do something different" to gain different results is challenging. But it must happen!

The second style of homebuilding is called *custom*. That is, the client engages a builder first and believes that they are building something special just for them (custom). My experience is that the same construction rules usually happen with the client only adding their preferred "cosmetic" surface choices. Thus, the quality difference of the home is not that significant. For example, when you are constructing a home design different than experience gained from previously built models, you have a tremendous set of variables that have to happen correctly again. In other words, you are betting that all those hand-fabricated parts, components purchased, different sub-contractors, etc., will all come together perfectly. Or as my old log-cabin expert, builder friend, would say "Every darn one of them is a prototype."

I want to plant a seed for a derivative of both of these building processes: *Semi-custom*. That is, a reasonable increase in technology that blends some higher-volume techniques like modularization of components, like SIPs, panelized walls, Timber Trusses, etc. and still allow some flexibility of style and regional tastes. It is fascinating in America that we migrate to this "throw-away mentality" of more and more high-volume, low cost gadgets. We want all of these features yet we do not build homes with the lessons learned from the high-tech industries, like electronics. Other countries are already migrating to this reality. Instead, we have all these cosmetic features, but the base-product quality is poor. I believe that this semi-custom process is particularly suited for addressing a large portion of the downsizing baby-boomers new homes since their range in size and style of the homes will be narrowed.

So where do we go from here? We must do more than "rearrange the furniture on the deck of the Titanic". We need to enter an age of moderation, of balance between thinking and feeling at his critical time. If you care to follow this path of discovery toward sanity, let's see if we can find an alternative to the Easter Island mentality.

02

Fundamentals of a Sane Last Home

Our goal at this initial phase of our journey is to establish the basics. I prefer to use the five base fundamentals listed below as the framework. In the following chapters, we evolve these fundamentals into several technical design/construction strategies that we will utilize to achieve an intelligent and more sane future home. The five fundamentals are:

    1 – Quality over Quantity

    2 – Sustainable Exterior

    3 – Low Energy Use

    4 – Owner's comfort first

    5 – Items 1-4 are linked to some

       degree

    Before expanding on each of these fundamentals, I want to explain a most basic operational process. We will strive to always make true apple/apple comparisons. We will fully compare values so we don't poise oranges against apples. Since we are aware that many of these fundamentals are somehow linked, this indicates that these comparison examples are innately more complex. Also, since our focus is on the baby-boomer's last homes, we will default more to the practical, rational side, rather than cosmetic issues. Frequently, practicality will be our tie-breaker. I request each of you make an honest attempt to balance your own cosmetic likes in a tie-breaker.

QUALITY OVER QUANTITY

The phrase "quality over quantity" is not new. But achieving this simple concept in the real-world of residential construction is almost always missed. Relating some examples of making specific decisions of these two variables will help. The most basic choice is simply the size of the home.

Since I want to assist the reader to visualize size, I'll start with a ratio of about 800 square feet (sq. ft.) per bedroom. Let's also, at this stage, only assume 2 bedrooms and 2 baths on one floor, with a technical reason and the resulting strategy fully explained later in Chapter 5. One good sanity check on this figure is that the new USGBC (U.S. Green Building Council) LEED for Homes certification process uses this 800 sq. ft./bedroom figure to gain the maximum points for *building green*. (If the house is larger, you are awarded less points.). Also, the EnergyStar Model home that we will dissect in detail in Chapter 12, was about 1,550 sq. ft.. Note that this particular model was built on a tight mountain lot and the base floor plan was originally at 1,650 sq. ft. The vast majority of weekend- and retirement-size homes are not far from this size since the U.S. national average home size for all residential units is about 2,000 sq. ft.

Now that we have something in the range of quantity, let's mate it with the second half of the fundamental. The quality side is that by choosing the size in this range, somewhat smaller than your prior home or even the national average, you establish a foothold. If you simply select a 10-20% larger house immediately in the initial planning stage, it seems to follow that your budget will be impacted. Too simple a concept? Almost every residential project misses this one! Set the goal of reasonable size with the idea that the resulting budget will allow using quality materials. Don't lock yourself into such a large size early that will constrain your budget when you near the end of construction.

One specific procedure that helps clients gauge this issue is by using what I call a *design guide*. It's a one-page sheet with a few questions for the client to answer about their new home wishes. Figure 2.1 is an example. When completed, even for just the main rooms, we have a simple chart of their old home room sizes and the future home's desired room sizes. When the client completes this form and adds up the two home versions, even after the typical initial goal of downsizing is stated, guess where the actual square footage summary takes them — *to reality!* They almost always end up close to their original home size. They want the master bedroom, the closets, the baths all similar. Thus, doing this exercise will focus on the baseline of size.

Another way to think about this quality-over-quantity concept is that during the actual process of building you can change some items to improve quality later, if your home size was reasonable at the beginning. However, almost all projects I have ever seen from any builder is that the client's budget gets squeezed as the project evolves (size was already large). You can't change sizing later in the construction cycle, so the quality of key components, for example, the roofing, gets compromised. 10% smaller can mean 10% better if you set sizing first.

SUSTAINABILE EXTERIOR

Our second fundamental, sustainable exterior, means a low-maintenance exterior on the home. This not only means less or no painting, it also implies that the materials selected will last (to avoid the dreaded replacement-cost factor). This long-lasting concept involves not only selecting high quality materials that don't rot or wear out, but how they are designed into each sub-assembly of the house. For example, if you use a high-quality, low-maintenance product like cement siding, but the trim design or the sub-assembly used has a high likelihood of leaking, then the high-quality item may be replaced by this design flaw issue. (Foreshadowing dormers!) Thus, keeping the design element details to a reasonable level of complexity is paramount.

A classic example of one portion of this concept working well, but another portion creating future havoc is the brick exterior/wood window trap. This brick home has the maintenance of re-painting the wood exterior windows in addition to the likelihood of replacement costs in the future, even after a few

HOME DESIGN GUIDELINES

CLIENT:_____   DATE:_____

CURRENT HOME	DIMENS.	S.F.	# WINDOWS	WIN. FACE	MISC.	TOTALS
# BEDROOMS						
# BATHS						
GREAT ROOM						
DINING						
MSTR. BEDRM						
2ND BEDROOM						
3RD BEDROOM						
LOFT/DEN						
MSTR. BATH						
MSTR. CLOSET						
BASEMENT ?						
GARAGE ?						
MISC.						
TOTALS						

LIKE BEST NOW?:   1. _____
                             2. _____
                             3. _____

NEW PROPERTY DESCRIPTION: _____

NEW PROPERTY LOCATION: _____

NEW HOME	DIMENS.	S.F.	# WINDOWS	WIN. FACE	MISC.	TOTALS
# BEDROOMS						
# BATHS						
GREAT ROOM						
DINING						
MSTR. BEDRM						
2ND BEDROOM						
3RD BEDROOM						
LOFT/DEN						
MSTR. BATH						
MSTR. CLOSET						
BASEMENT ?						
GARAGE ?						
MISC.						
TOTALS						

WANT IN NEW HOME?: 1. _____
                                2. _____
                                3. _____

Art Smith • Rocky Ridge Designs • rockyridge@ellijay.com • 706-635-8555 • www.rockyridgedesigns.com

Figure 2.1 Home design guidelines

paintings. Due to the more complex task of painting the wood exterior windows on a brick home, I have seen even this cost equal up to 50% of painting the entire house. The windows need to be a higher quality. The goal is having the *entire* exterior as sustainable as your budget allows. (We chose to make it "less bigger", correct?)

LOW ENERGY USE

The next fundamental, low energy use, has been on most homeowner's minds since the first major energy crisis in the 1970s. Moving beyond wishes to achieve this target works best if you set defined and recognized standards. A good starting point for outlining specific steps is the EPA's *EnergyStar* guidelines. Newer local building codes are a starting point for the average home, but the EnergyStar approach is a significant level above the typical code minimum. Also, the USGBC's *LEED For Homes* program utilizes the EnergyStar Guidelines as a prerequisite. Most of us, with the modern saturation of advertising, now know about EnergyStar, but the media focus is on CFL light bulbs, refrigerators and dishwashers. These help reduce energy costs, but our focus is on higher insulating standards for the home's *building envelope*, which is the insulating quality of the entire house.

The areas of focus of the building envelope are:
- Low infiltration exterior (low leakage, minimal holes)
- Superior wall- and roof-insulating products (quality)
- Higher insulation levels with more R-value (quantity)
- Better grade of windowa (higher R-value, or lower "U")
- Better grade of exterior doors
- Better roof envelope design (non-vented over vented roof)

OWNER'S COMFORT FIRST

This concept is so basic that almost everyone believes they are exercising this already. They are not even close! This comfort means that the home's day-to-day living functions take priority over the curb-appeal issues. A good scene to ponder is thinking where one will spend the majority of their time. Will you be sitting in the street admiring your house after bedtime? Will you still be sitting

there, after the realtor told you on your first visit how much curb appeal your new house will have? Do you want huge windows at the street side so everybody can see your daily activities while driving by? Or do you want windows to see the special view (soft-touch) that was important to you upon buying your new property? Do you want extra protruding gables or bay windows that are catchy at the curb but expensive to build and difficult to use because of the small space? Do you want tall windows that are attractive, but let in so much sun in the summer that the room is not useful? Do you want so much imperfect symmetry in window and door patterns that real furniture will not fit in the room?

Specific topics for weighing to achieve comfort are:
- A simple-flowing and open floor plan
- Windows sized and placed for practical use
- Utilizing proper day lighting
- Door sizes and locations carefully chosen
- Minimize the impact of stair location
- Minimize halls
- Ceiling sizes reasonable but not for a "warehouse"
- Adequate fresh air control when desired (not leaks)
- Interior finishes that don't contribute to indoor pollution
- Radon protection?

ITEMS 1-4 ARE LINKED TO A DEGREE

The last fundamental is simply that most of the first four are interrelated in some way and some are intensely linked.

By the way, whose house are you building anyway? The realtor's? The banker's, the general contractor's or the sub-contractor's? Ask yourself if resale value is an issue for your last home ? Are these people going to be around when you have to paint and fix the choices that they influenced? Will they bring you warm blankets on a cold New England night or a cool drink when the Southern sun is at its peak? They won't, so let's find out how to prepare for us.

03

Less is More

The technique for breaking the vicious cycle of rationalizing that one can have every cosmetic detail and feature is to ask the question, "Who will be making the payments on the proposed dream house?" During the emotional phase of planning and building a home this fact is usually lost. The bottom line is the *bottom line*: If you use more material, it will either  be of a lower quality or you need more finances (however, there is a dollar limit somewhere) to maintain the quality level. A realistic analogy lies in the learning experience that young people have as they learn to use charge cards. The instant gratification of the momentary purchase fades in one's memory until the monthly bill arrives. Then the shock hits that we bought the item in question and we now have to write out the check to cover the purchase. In

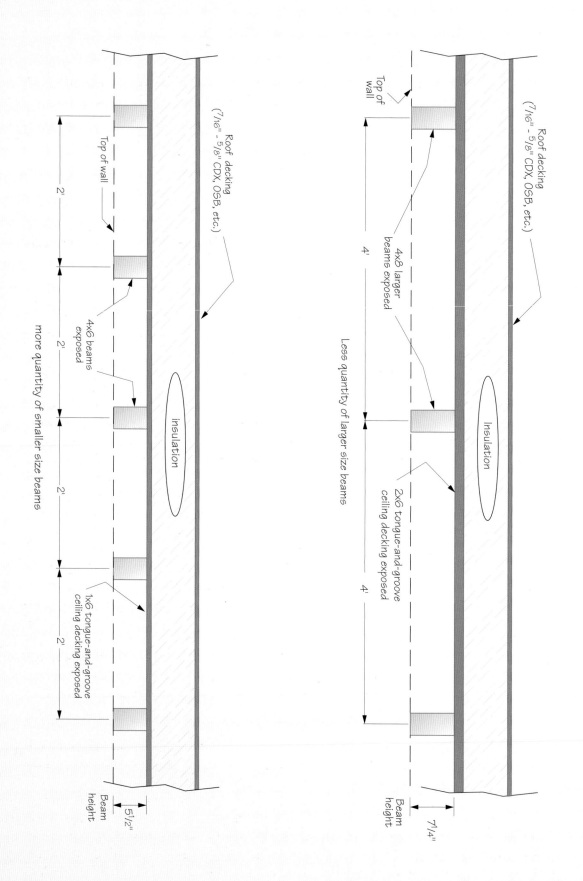

Figure 3.1 4×6 roof beams on 2' centers

Figure 3.2 4×8 roof beams on 4' centers

the later stages of homebuilding, this scenario hits the owner frequently with the little reminder of those "extras we added". A difficult wake-up call!

One principle that is interwoven with less-is-more is the reality of trade-offs or compromises — you gain something if you give something else. This concept seems to be missing in current American life. Those of us with backgrounds in engineering and building high-volume products live with this regimen daily. A good macro-level version of this is that everyone has a final budget on a home-construction project — even Bill Gates — but a real figure exists. Thus, compromises must occur. Using less-is-more is intended as a key technique to find the best set of trade-offs.

Before we apply less-is-more to technical steps, a comparison of two different home decisions will help. At the time we were building our future North Georgia cabin, planned much earlier for retirement, our friend with the McMansion toy playroom (dining room) had just purchased this new larger home. We were discussing some of the home details that were available to buyers as options. I noticed that a large number of homes had the three-sided brick detail. Three sides of the home viewed from the street were brick, but the rear of the house was a lower grade of siding. In order to add the brick to the fourth side, the extra cost was about $8,500. Ironically, our choice of a rustic brick for the bulk of the exterior (with some stone zones) for our little mountain cabin was about this same amount; combining the brick mason's labor and the brick material cost. The two family's needs and situations are different, but this points to the less-is-more strategy's usefulness. Because I was covering less area I was able to use a better material. If my friend still lived in that house, the repainting of that fourth lower-grade wall (maybe twice by now) would be approaching the brick's original cost.

A derivative of less-is-more applies to both the structural and cosmetic decision processes. A structural example that fits our own region is the timber-style structure — use larger components and less of them. Instead of hand cutting several smaller pieces of wood or using smaller trusses, use a few larger trusses. There are other factors, tied to the structural style one chooses, that can be missed. For example, even if you didn't choose the casual timber look, typical hand-framing of the roof requires other steps to finish, not including the waste, labor time, etc.

Let's assume that the client wants a casual wood ceiling look. They could use 4×6 exposed-beam rafters at 2' spacings and 1×6 tongue-and-groove decking or larger 4×8 beams with thicker 2×6 decking at a wider spacing of 4'. (Compare Figures 3.1 and 3.2.) Not considering the other hidden factors that each choice determines, the larger-beam-less-quantity choice usually works better. (Sometimes the cheaper 1×6 decking forces other design limitations, such as insulation technologies not available in the cheaper structural choice.)

Another example of this less-is-more concept is considering how many windows to have on one wall. My suggestion is that three large windows are better than four standard-sized windows. This appearance-only decision has several hidden levels. First, the worker has to frame more openings in the structure. Despite any rationalization of ways a framing sub-contractor may price the job, it will cost more. More trim and finishing on both the outside and inside are required. Pertaining to energy design, there are more places for air infiltration to occur. In higher volume building processes delved into later, the cost is higher. The pattern of the three windows is that the two outer windows can be a higher-quality casement venting windows that flank a larger, fixed-pane, non-venting window.

Figure 3.3 and Figure 12.8 (it's okay to peek ahead), show the view that is available using the three-window pattern. My experience shows that this larger, fixed window's original cost is similar to the smaller, flanking venting windows. Also, this larger, fixed window will typically have a better insulating value. Thus, a more desirable lower U-value (higher insulating R-value) is achieved at a lower cost. The clincher is that this less-chopped-up window scheme fits the basic goal of a window: you can see something when you look out. (This is significant if these windows are on the *view* side or passive-solar South side of the house). Less windows units mean more utility, better dollar value and better energy value. Sometimes linked values are not easily discovered.

An important sub-concept to this triple-window idea is that it follows the less-is-more idea. It can be enticing to change this window pattern to access to the deck outside (typical on weekend-style cabins) under the guise of gaining direct access to the deck. Several trade-offs come into play. First, a door of a similar high-quality design will cost more, factoring in higher glass-content. Second, the air infiltration issue becomes difficult to manage and the window pattern becomes awkward. For example, one of the flanking windows will now have a door occupying that space. Now there are three different size elements in one wall section. Third, the important view side is interrupted.

Using a door or a tall window here is an example of the compounding effect of the inter-related values of a decision. A door and a window are not the same. A door's location impacts the traffic flow in the room and you can't use the space at the bottom of the door. With a mid-level height window, say 54" tall, you can usually place some lower furniture, a bookcase, etc. in this lower zone without impacting the window's primary functions of light, view and air flow. Both a tall window and a door have this penalty. You needed more airflow and the door is not as useful as the venting side windows. Since we are dealing with more space-efficient homes, maximizing the functionality of each space is paramount. The funny thing about this larger window/door choice is what I call the beach-rental-view syndrome. Have you ever been on a beach vacation, either at a high-rise condominium or a quaint little beach cottage? They usually share a common physical trait. They likely have a deck/patio with a railing, facing the beach. When you look at this huge, sliding patio door or a tall window, what is your view? (You've probably figured this one out already.) You have a terrific view of the railing and the decking material (knotting and twisting wood decking) not the ocean. What have you gained with the larger vertical window/door? (This sliding patio door technique is replicated in weekend cabins in the master bedroom. There's another *minor* detail. It is the *only* window/door combination in the room. If you desire some fresh air, will you leave the door open?)

One principle that is interwoven with less-is-more is the reality of trade-offs or compromises — you gain something if you give something else.

I have a personal experience of a similar door choice. Since I tend to 'pioneer" many building concepts, ideas and techniques in my own homes over the years, I also, unfortunately, find some of the follies. This time, despite all of my best planning and thinking, in our mountain cabin master bedroom, we had the large-window view (also for passive solar reasons it was south facing) as the main window element. I pushed the height so this main window was 6' wide and 5' feet high. It was a majestic view from the fixed picture window. To achieve both the egress and ventilating needs, I had to do two extra things.

First, a small awning window was squeezed under the big picture window and a full-glass door was installed adjacent to the big window. I fully understood the trade-offs before committing to this design. Second, we selected high-quality windows and a door from a respected supplier. Murphy's Law surfaced after about ten-year's of use. Due to the more complex installation around the masonry/deck area and despite having a good contractor install them, two leaks appeared, one in the window and one in the door base. The window seal failure was a freak statistical failure, but likely our high-mountain and windy and wetter environment accelerated this defect. The door had a caulking failure. The resulting water-damage repair costs to the structure were close to the main components original costs. The realization was (considered at the decision stage) we rarely used the door to go out to the deck. If I had chosen the triple-window combination, I likely would not have had this problem. Another element of more value to ponder: With the triple-window style, we could have added a window-seat nook in front of the window design. We now know that this choice would have been "more" (value).

Another client's experience with the window choice demonstrates how this simple decision negated much of the client's key goal. The house

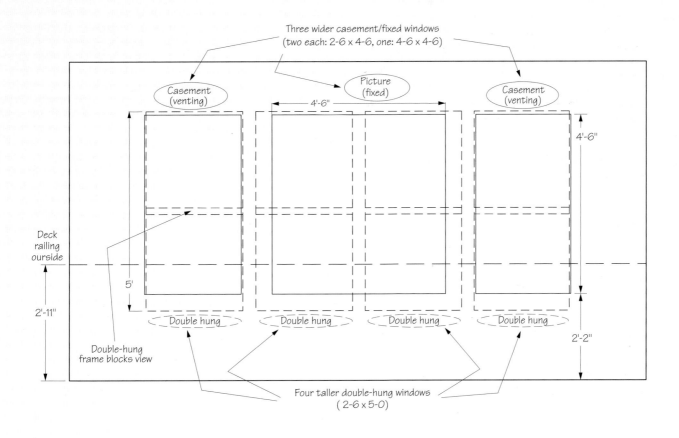

Three wider casement/fixed windows
(two each: 2-6 x 4-6, one: 4-6 x 4-6)

Casement
(venting)

Picture
(fixed)

Casement
(venting)

4'-6"

4'-6"

Deck
railing
ourside

5'

2'-11"

Double hung

Double hung

Double hung

Double hung

2'-2"

Double-hung
frame blocks view

Four taller double-hung windows
(2-6 x 5-0)

Figure 3.3 Three windows vs. four windows.

design's main thrust was to optimize the view of the lot toward a small lake across the road from the building site. The geography of the lot lead to the decision to face the narrow, gabled end of the house toward the lake. This gable end contained the chimney from the great room end. This open plan had the living room, the kitchen and the dining room clustered in this end of the house, with the fireplace centered in the gable. Flanking the central fireplace (to be rock covered) were two large, fixed-pane, non-venting windows to maximize the view to the lake, as depicted in my original drawings for the client. Each window was about 6' wide and 4'-6" high (important technical detail later on this height). What was built were two, double-hung, 5'-high windows occupying each of the large window zones. It took four windows to fill up the space of the two larger ones. This revised window pattern killed the original goal of having a view of the lake. Despite the fact that this was a spec house and the window budget was lower than I typically advise the client to use, the four windows cost more than

the two larger ones. And, other technical hassles appeared out of this choice.

Due to the good window design elsewhere in the room, both adequate venting (fresh air potential) and the egress issues were covered. (Egress code states that another opening other than the entry door, typically a window, must provide a 24"-high by 20"-wide opening for escape or rescue.) If the four windows had met egress code, they would have been taller, likely 5'-2". Since the installed windows were closer to the floor, they should have had the added tempered-glass safety cost. (The large fixed ones also required tempered glass.) Since that construction, our state codes have mandated even stricter rules for windows at this height above the outside grade for the safety of small children. The bottom line was the original two large picture window units would have provided the view desired, provided privacy from the road, have been more energy efficient and cost less. Thus, less quantity of windows delivered more value across multiple factors. Diligence!

A recent, large-deck project comes to mind. The client's intentions on this new home were to strive for a low-maintenance exterior. However, during the design meetings with the client, I noted that the deck size, particularly connecting walkways on the sides were growing. After the contractor completed the decks, which were divided by a central porch section, and the connecting side walkways, the size had really grown. They used a low-maintenance product for the deck's surface, but the resulting railing length was large. For budget reasons, the railings installed were pressure-treated wood, rather than the low-maintenance decking. The trade-off question is, "Will the larger deck space be worth the future maintenance costs of the lower-cost railings?" Less decking size and features would have been more hassle free. Diligence about getting or not getting bigger at the point of decision is crucial.

The classic structural (or let's say practical) vs. cosmetic trade-off happens frequently. The goal of this deck framing technique was to minimize the cosmetic joints (end joints of length) of the surface decking. The chosen, low maintenance decking went perpendicular to the house side (for look). The 20'-long material would be cut in half for the deck's 10' depth out from the house and there would not be any joints seen at the lengths of the decking. This meant that the supporting floor joists under the decking, typically at 16" centers, needed to run parallel to the house or deck. This then required that the structural girders connecting these parallel joists be at 8' to 10' spacing. These main structural girders are attached to the house's ledger board at only seven to nine locations. If they had attached each of the 16"-spaced, 10'-long joists, rotated 90° out from the house, directly to the house, with proper joist hangers, the result would have been forty to fifty points of contact to tie into the house. The deck framed for cosmetics would likely meet the *minimum* structural safety code, but the more conservative design is more (value and safety). Figure 3.4 shows this conservative framing approach for a 30'-wide deck. The bottom line is that the cosmetic look to minimize visual joints overcame the conservative structural design techniques. Note: The longer 20' lengths of high-quality synthetic decking would have had less joints and would not bow and twist like the typical 16' pressure-treated wood decking.

This deck structural/look decision confirms one of my design rules. There is usually some structural (or rational) price to pay for a cosmetic detail (emotional look). Look for this hidden monster. Once you have discovered and understand this trade off, you will be able to design around it or eliminate it. This does not mean that if the client desires this feature to immediately drop it, but be ready to move forward with developing a better solution.

A frustrating example of less-is-more was prompted by the efforts of a builder to dress up the exterior of another house. Note that this home is well-built, with a Timber Truss interior, SIP wall construction, high-grade windows, energy-efficient techniques, etc. How did less-is-more mess this up, as one friend who drives by this home daily said, "They ruined it"? The planned exterior of the home was to utilize a long-life, cement-based shingle. This product required painting, but would last and also blend with the general appearance of the neighborhood. At the last day, before installing these shingles, with the material at the site, the builder decided to change the exterior. His decision to use a low-maintenance, *vinyl shingle* seemed well placed. However, when he priced shingling the gable ends of the house, the waste factor almost doubled the cost. They then chose the low-cost vinyl lap siding for all but the front, center section of the house. Here they used the higher-priced vinyl shingles. Due to the building's shape, as you drove by you could easily see the two main gables of the large, front center plus the two smaller gable ends at the ends of the house. The beige-colored, vinyl lap siding was not only different than the gray, front shingles, but was immediately recognized as "cheap vinyl siding". Beige J-trim strips used with the vinyl siding were around the windows (which had a high-grade, hunter-green, aluminum-clad exterior already installed). Some of the other house trim was also hunter green. By the time it was completed, this large number of different colors likely did not mesh (in my opinion). The original, simple, color scheme would have been "more".

Ironically, about three years after this project was completed, I was at a nearby-friend's birthday party. She introduced me to her local realtor friend who had recently toured the multi-colored house. The realtor, to my gratification, asked, "Why did the builder use so many colors on the outside of the house?" Yes, less would have been best.

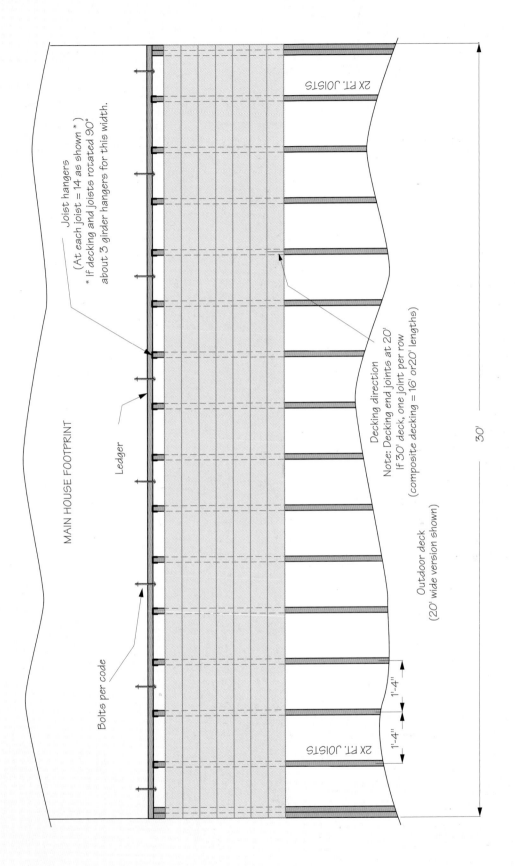

Figure 3.4 Conservative deck framing.

The Curb-Appeal Penalty

Americans are so enamored with realtor comments, magazine articles and TV shows that stress only the

appearance of the house from the street, that we have distorted comfort and a home's primary function. In fact, most of the fix-it-up-to-sell shows or articles frequently focus on curb appeal. I suggest that this approach is dangerous for baby-boomer's homes of the future. We are striving to capture the *wow factor* and another *wow*, called bankruptcy, is growing. We are building houses with all-show and no-go. Let's look at some characteristics of currently in-style homes and identify the price we pay.

A new trend, already alluded to earlier, is the focus on high-pitched roofs. This resulting size can be dramatic when viewed from the street. The cost factor for increasing the roof pitch for appearance is detailed in

Figure 4.1. A chart summarizing the increased roof area to be shingled is included. For this curb-appeal discussion, let's assume that a steep 12/12 roof pitch has about 25 percent longer rafter lengths than a medium 6/12 roof pitch. This means that you will have 25 percent more roofing area to shingle, not to mention that the whole roof structure is larger. Top sheathing plywood/OSB (if you use a typical spec house, lower cost vented roof design), the sheathing covering (tar paper), nails and labor costs all increase. A hidden factor may come into play that "common sense" might miss. If the rafter length is 25 percent longer, common sense implies that this piece of wood needs to be 25 percent longer. No. Structural design guidelines state that this 2×6 rafter on the 6/12 roof may have to be, say, a 2×8 rafter. This is a geometric, or squaring ratio, similar to the braking distance of a car. (At 60mph, a car, with maximum braking, will need about 150' to stop. With a 10mph speed increase, the braking distance is closer to 200'.) Thus, our "only a 25 percent increase" will cost more than that.

How does all this detail relate to curb-appeal? You *do* have a larger roof area being presented to the street. But, since you are using a typically-constructed, vented roof design with asphalt shingles, roof life is a valid question. My experience has shown that the average shingle life is about one-half of the *rated* shingle life.

The typical shingle is rated with a 25-year life span. At around 12 years, asphalt roof shingles will not look good and fading occurs even earlier. My empirical experience in the hotter, Southern United States climate is that this actual life figure is even worse. I have driven by hundreds of neighborhoods for ten to more than thirty years and I challenge anyone to not confirm this fact. An interesting American trend of this last generation: During their fast-changing, on-the-go, high-tech, multi-tasking careers and lives, Americans are moving about every seven years. They aren't around long enough to see this phenomenon! Nor are the builders around either.

Let's go back to the *look* of the roof shingles. A 25 percent cost savings means a higher-grade shingle can be used that will look better in future years. Increases in better grades of asphalt shingles is about 8-10 percent per stage. Thus, a 30-year shingle costs about 10 percent more than a 20-year shingle, a 40 year is 10 percent more than the 30-year shingle, etc. A 40-year *architectural-style* shingle looks better and is 25-30 percent more in material costs than the typical 25-year shingle, but labor is about the same. Much of our population is living in homes with the older, lower-grade 20-year asphalt shingles. Oh yes, the replacement asphalt shingle is an oil-based product, really compounding this global burden.

Did we really improve the look by going with a steeper roof? We *will* have more area, but with a lower-quality shingle to look at. I submit that by choosing an improved-quality shingle and a reasonable roof pitch, the aesthetic gain is better than being larger. Longer-life roofing material like concrete tile or standing-seam metal roofs are good choices. (See Chapter 6.) The basic function of a roof is to protect the structure of the building. Is your home still pretty if the roof leaks and water damage/mold/mildew results?

From the street, it's difficult to gauge the ceiling height. Part of this is a lingering effect of the "fad" of us used to seeing taller houses so much lately. That is, the peer pressure of building similar in the neighborhood makes the roof heights similar or they will stand out as dated, or out-of-style. For example, the 6/12 average roof pitch example stated appears to be somewhat flatter, than the norm in the neighborhood. But as we will see in the next chapter, another factor is occurring inside this particular house that is very significant. But at this time, please accept that when clients actually go inside this 6/12 house and see the almost 15 high cathedral ceiling (hint), they think that this height is wonderful! But, when they see a "normal" 12/12 pitch roof, like in a Mountain Chalet or new England Cape Cod that looks now "normal" from the street, guess what the reaction inside is? The resulting 22 foot or so ridge peak is really too tall if you are standing inside under the full "open" cathedral zone! Thus, the inside and outside evaluations don't match. However, the often-chosen compromise is simply for street look only.

Another related roof topic is my earlier noted "Six-foot rule". Thus, the tendency in modern subdivisions to simply complicate the roof to extremes. Now without going to another painful analysis like the roof rafter length only, can the reader begin to understand the increase in cost? Yes, the extra labor

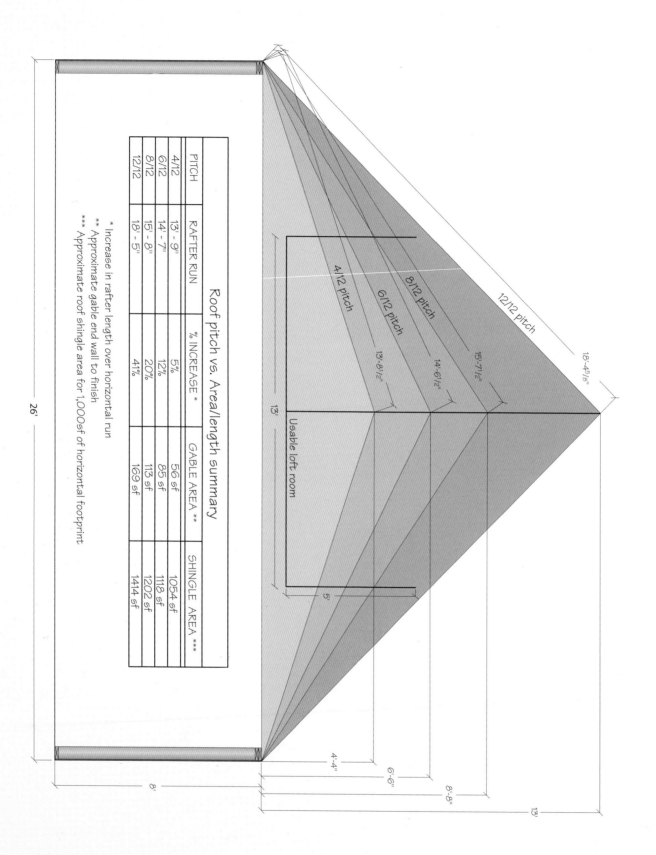

Roof pitch vs. Area/length summary

PITCH	RAFTER RUN	% INCREASE *	GABLE AREA **	SHINGLE AREA ***
4/12	13' - 9"	5%	56 sf	1054 sf
6/12	14 - 7"	12%	85 sf	1118 sf
8/12	15' - 8"	20%	113 sf	1202 sf
12/12	18' - 5"	41%	169 sf	1414 sf

* Increase in rafter length over horizontal run
** Approximate gable end and wall to finish
*** Approximate roof shingle area for 1,000sf of horizontal footprint

Figure 4.1 The roof-pitch penalty

and materials for each design change feature adds up rapidly. Thus, these cosmetic design features put even more pressure on the budget to even buy higher quality shingles. Another compounding factor is that the more complex roofs are even more likely to leak even with the base quality of the components remaining the same. For example, I have seen many conflicting gables or vertical walls so close together that they will beg for problems. One example is a large front gable entry porch ending at the roof, almost touching a side wall of a loft dormer side. Thus, this large roof area is collecting water and literally funneling this volume to this one small point. Check with reputable roofing contractors. They like this growing backlog of future business! You will pay them directly later ("The Penalty") for the perceived increase in curb appeal.

A specific design element, dormers, to the extreme that I call ""dormeritus"", was raised earlier. It is important to note this specific feature's compounding of the above already complicated roof design. In fairness, dormers have some very basic positive design assets, particularly in two story homes (when absolutely required to be two story). A well-designed dormer can make a tight second floor space useful. However, even the best designs have other cosmetic negatives. First, think about the complexities of gutters on a typical "doghouse" style dormer. The two short eaves on either side of the protruding gable could, or should have gutters. If you have gutters, then getting the drain pipe off the roof to the ground is tricky and usually unsightly ("LOOK" penalty). If you avoid the gutter downspout, but still have the gutters, you have a concentration of water in a small zone. The cosmetic drain problem of this solution on the actual roof shingles is frequently observed. But, the higher concentration of water will likely increase the chance of future leaks. Even on the protruding gable end (the side principally seen from the street), with the other gutter issues either solved or avoided has another appearance issue. This issue particularly shows up in wood-sided "cabins". That

is, the real splash problem causes a discoloration of the siding at the base of the dormer at the roof intersection, typically a foot or so above the shingles. I have observed many examples of this, even with a good exterior stain as early as one year after this coating! This is not a curb-appeal positive. By the way, I'm not climbing up there to re-paint this zone! Are you?

A past re-modeling project of one of my subcontractor friends really indicates the severity of the time penalty for a design feature of a dormer.

Sort of: "Seventeenth floor, everything is OK...." This very accomplished crew took on a remodeling project, on their own, between major framing projects for general contractors. They bought an approximately 30 year-old home to re-model and re-sell. This "almost" two-story home had a large dormer upstairs providing, a more useful zone for, I believe, the upstairs bath. While visiting the crew one day, a few days after significant demolition was accomplished, I had one of those "This Old House" moments of discovery. That is, as I was first walking through the living room area, on the main floor, I noticed that this floor system was sagging. Now my excellent framer friends had noted this already and had even had determined the culprit. The dormer above and to the rear of the house had been leaking for years and the flowing water finally collected, after a rambling journey through the home structural core, on the first floor joists. These structural members rotted over time with the loss of strength. Besides the obvious, initially observed, tarnished cosmetic clues of the decayed roof area right at the dormer, this other extremely significant penalty resulted. It was observed that this particular design did not include many of the "better practices" of flashing techniques, etc. However, I believe that many similar examples, to even a lesser degree, exist out there and are lurking with their own time-released surprise.

But if you must have to have a dormer, for natural lighting or some appearance reason, go with what I call a gable dormer as indicated in Figure

Longer-life roofing materials like concrete tile or standing-seam metal roofs are good choices.

4.2. Note that only one medium size unit Vs two smaller ones (LESS/MORE) is the better operational mode. The resulting roof intersections of this style are simple and appear as a roof valley and do not have the "doghouse" dormer side-walls and the associated gutter issues (not needed with this design). I also would continue our simple guidelines by keeping the visible interior cut into the roof a rectangle shape, slightly larger than the rectangle window, and not the natural triangular exterior roof footprint of the this dormer type. Care must also be exercised regarding the sun-shading of the dormer window, particularly on the South and West sides. (See Chapter 9 for window and sun orientation details) However, note that I would even consider a high-quality, smaller skylight as an alternative over even this gable dormer version. It is recognized that skylights allow about four times the light in than a vertical window. (Note: preferably not on South side of house.)

One curb-appeal generality that is so compelling, it really is hard to change. That is, the need to have the most of windows facing the street is so significant that I also struggle with this decision. In a typical subdivision, this pull is necessary for architectural similarity, resale value, curb-appeal in general and so on. I add that a specially designed last home is likely not in a typical subdivision, but one that is more dictated by view, more rustic and demanding site (mountain or lake), where the front of the house rules are at least minimal or non existent. Realizing that some active-adults-over-55 subdivisions may be closer to the mid-life suburban situation, I still think some moderation of this pull is useful. For example, if the homes principal view side, with typical geography dictating the road and driveway locations, is usually away from the road. Then, the larger windows desired for seeing this view will likely be away from the road (details in the next chapter). Thus, the bathroom, closets and lower function rooms will likely be closer to the road, or entry side of the home. The tendency is thus to add abnormally large windows in these small rooms due to our accustomed appearance of suburbia. The penalty is that this window size, besides the actual window cost, distorts the room's usefulness. This is a tricky one, so let's save the details for Chapter 5. Just be aware for now that there is a trade off hidden with this choice.

A similar concept to window location is depicted in one of my best one-size-fits-all stories. This particular home design has been built many times in a particular development. That is, the builder's evolved formula was this exact plan replicated in a variety of lots and resulting different terrains. Specifically, the front porch always faced the road with a deck on an adjacent side. When built on this observed site, the porch obviously faced the road. Thus, if you occupied this porch, you had only the road to admire. The deck, for outside living needs, was 90° around one side. The deck view here was really only one of the neighbor's deck. Oh, by the way, one of the most majestic North Georgia wilderness mountain ranges can be viewed from this lot. However it really can't be seen from this porch or this deck as located. A few reasonably large windows are on this view side of the mountain range, but most of the larger windows have a great view of the road! Yes, it has a prominent dormer on the road side (with a loft zone and a big window) and yes it also has this tarnished splash pattern at the dormer gable base. And no, I won't get up there to re-stain this one. I trust that this set of penalties is now fairly obvious.

An interesting epilogue to the lack of view above came from a potential client. This client approached me with a lot of the issues that have already been discussed. He also owned this exact floor plan, but located in a different part of the project. Now retired for only a few years, he sited maintenance of this attractive, curb-appealing style as his main worry. The emotional dilemma he faced is that his wife really liked the house (curb appeal) and did not want to move. We talked a few times, he investigated some alternatives, but never actually engaged with moving forward with his new retirement home desire. The validity demonstrated here is that a real family, with the exact home design, was already experiencing this pain just a few years into the retirement phase. When I drove by his home, I spotted several structural issues that they will deal with later, probably sooner than he realizes. (Hint: Wood decks with the base of the posts in the ground.)

Moving on, we will see that basic geometry decisions have major repercussions if we are not smart.

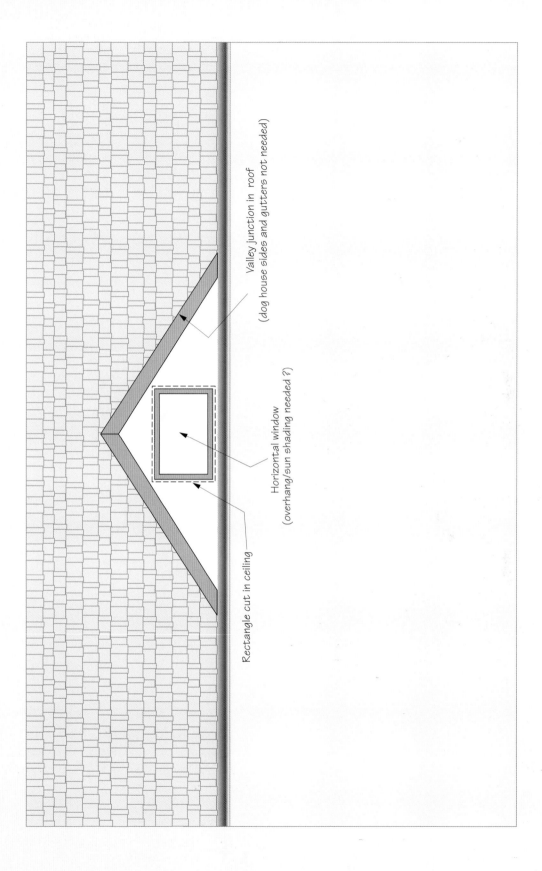

Valley junction in roof
(dog house sides and gutters not needed)

Horizontal window
(overhang/sun shading needed?)

Rectangle cut in ceiling

Figure 4.2 Gable dormer

Go Horizontal, Not Vertical

Two things that stand out in the McMansion houses are multi-story designs and the exaggerated roof pitches.

We have already discussed how both contribute to hidden costs, decrease options, add to the maintenance burden and it is more difficult to achieve lower energy usage. Let's expand on a retiring-baby-boomer's building strategy for homes that are similar to early ranch-style houses. But this is not your ordinary ranch.

One maxim that applies to almost all technologies and life experiences, particularly to developing a product, is K.I.S.S. (Keep It Simple Stupid). Despite current, popular sayings like "thinking outside the box", most successful projects or products are the result of good, "limited scope" management. One comment countering the outside the box phrase is: "If you think outside the box, you may miss what's inside it." Keeping the house design basic is good. The first step is to have *one main level* for your future home. Most of these homes will be located in sloping lots where a basement is likely to be built, so this single-main-floor concept will need modification. A hybrid approach of the Chalet version follows at the end of this chapter.

Let's assume that a basement is in the plans and that the first floor area is about 1,600 sq. ft. This is larger than our childhood home size of around 1,000 sq. ft. that typically had three bedrooms and one bath. (In the United States now, the average-size house doubles our childhood size.)

If we are building on sloped property, simple geometry dictates that the basic shape of the house should be what I call a soft rectangle. In Figure 5.1, you'll see that one side of the house is up the hill. The downhill side will have a daylight basement area.

When the grader is working on a sloping slot, unless the lot has a plateau at the top, they will have to do significant digging out of the natural terrain at *both* the basement and above the house. This *above* zone, the second cut, has several issues related to the garage location and an environmental impact. As the depth of the house approaches 30', the basement is close to coming out of the ground. This means a stable and expensive structure, like sub-walls (reinforced concrete walls) below the basement floor will be needed. Going further down the hill, the depth of the deck location compounds this problem because the deck's mounting posts are getting taller. Not only are they are increasing in height, they may need to grow from 4×4 to 6×6 wood posts, or more expensive steel columns. Also, more

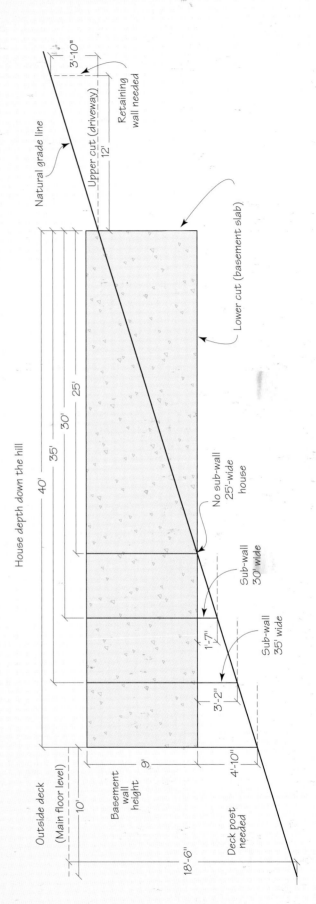

Figure 5.1 Effect of lot slope on foundation

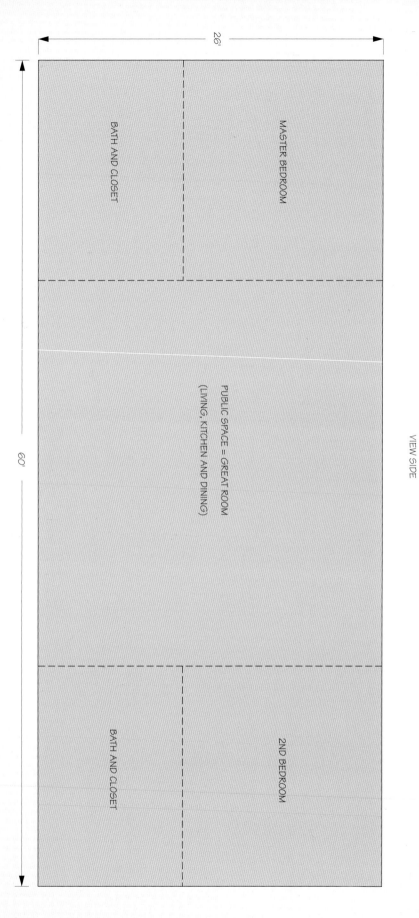

Figure 5.2 Simplified floor plan

diagonal bracing for the longer posts and the deck is needed. Our standard Timber Truss sizes were selected for the 20' to 26' range, enabling respectable room sizes but they wont' bear the burden of this terrain-dictating expense.

Let's say that the basic rectangle shape of your new home is 26' wide by 60' long. Figure 5.1 can't depict the third dimension of "rotation". The terrain's slope on the lot is at some other angle, rotated more than shown, because the house won't fit parallel to the terrain's ridgeline of slope. In other words, the house's position starts behaving more like a large square than a rectangle. This means that the base shape of the rectangle should help minimize the sub-wall. Likely a small sub-wall, at the lowest corner, will result, but minimizing this issue at the beginning is important.

A square vs. a rectangle comparison should clear up this concept. One prospective client approached me to design their retirement home. My first fear was realized when they had seen a picture in a well-known magazine and had fallen in love with the "look". They already owned the building site near the top of a mountain, with steep slope and rock issues, which had terrific potential for a majestic mountain view. I sent them an e-mail outlining some of the issues and mailed them a drawing similar to Figure 5.1. They also had an initial concept by another designer. Both of the designs were a 40' by 40' square. Figure 5.1 shows that the basement, decks, etc. are in space. What was later designed and built by someone else was better than the 40' by 40' square, but it was still almost 32' deep and 40' wide with two stories on the basement. If the 40' width is oriented toward the view side, this means you only have 40' of width to maximize your view using windows, doors, etc. Note also my proposed 26' by 60' rectangle shape would have fit very well on the terrain. During construction, the above-ground rock resulted in about 6' of subsurface rock to be excavated for the basement's 32' depth down the hill. I can only guess how much this line item cost, but several days of using a big excavator with a rock-smasher head must have been expensive. The basement sub-wall then averaged 8' high along most of the 40' section. Also, this zone needs to be properly filled by packing the material and strengthening the basement slab floor (it would have been "up in the air"). Almost any width house

would have had some sub-wall for this site. For the direct and indirect costs (and later in the garage section), my estimate is that several thousand dollars was added to the cost of the house.

The next step is to fill in this rectangular shape with two bedrooms, two baths and a common public area, consisting of a great room (or living room), kitchen and dining area. (See Figure 5.2.) Keep things simple, the public areas are grouped into one larger, open zone called the great room. You can imagine the millions of different floor plans that are out there. However, in the end, there are only a few basic shapes with minor differences. If you decide on the rectangle concept, this narrows the variations. I suggest that the great room be in the middle and the bedrooms and baths at each end of the house. I refer to these bedrooms as the bedroom wings. (See Figure 5.2.) You have seen, probably lived in and/or designed other variations of this space but, in my experience, this is a good beginning point for a new home.

If you are already retired, you are most likely a couple with children that have moved out of the nest. The need to have the convenience of one-level living is accepted universally at this stage of your life. With the second bedroom at the opposite end from the master bedroom, the second bedroom can be furnished as an office and/or a guest bedroom with a fold-out-bed or small love seat. This allows for a good flow in the great room. Figure 12.1 shows that two bedroom wings have doors that open almost directly to the great room. The second bedroom wing, with public access to the second bath, has a hall area of about 4' by 4'. We've "wasted" only 16 sq. ft. of overhead for this hall space. In smaller homes, this efficiency is needed. Flashback to our 1960's childhood ranch homes. Also, wider halls are recommended for retirement-age living.

My "double-hall-penalty" rule is a fundamental floor plan strategy. I was asked to look over some house plans with the idea of adding some key structural, energy efficient, low maintenance suggestions. The clients were planning to build their retirement home in a rural site with a less-formal, downsized, open floor plan. Their plan essentially worked that way. However, I spotted an issue with the master closet area. They wanted to put their customized dresser in the center of the master closet, which cluttered up the closet and created a double hall. Figure 5.3 shows an average-size walk-in closet. If the dresser or custom built-in base cabinet is placed in the center, you can see the double-hall penalty. There will be a 3'-wide hallway on either side of the dresser and about 2' for each clothes-hanging zone. (This wider-version closet is shown in the bottom half of Figure 5.3.) A 70 sq. ft. closet has grown to 120 sq. ft.. The 3'-wide hall zone needs to be at the end of the closet as well as a clearance zone near the entry door. So, a 10' depth has been reduced to 4'. What is the penalty for doing this? The extra 50 sq. ft. of floor space for the double hall would cost about $5000. This is assuming a relatively modest cost of $100/sq. ft. Wow what a penalty! Better be a nice dresser in there!

How else could this $5000 be spent? The roof could be upgraded to standing seam metal or granite countertops. Usually, this $5000 was not planned for, so the hit usually comes by subtracting quality from somewhere else.

One more thing — the middle dresser not only increased the main-level floor space, it increased the roofing area, and, even worse, the basement space. In two story homes, this is even more costly.

Compare the floor plans in Figure 5.4 and Figure 5.5. Both are 1000 sq. ft. houses with a three bedroom layout with only one bath in both cases. Compare the improvement in size of the two smaller bedrooms by eliminating the hall. For these examples, typical 2×4 wall framing and ½" sheetrock is figured for the interior so we can see the actual area left for these two rooms. The dimensions are to the nearest inches and area is to the nearest square feet. The closets are identical in area, but not the same shapes, so you can see the differences in the bedrooms.

In Fig. 5.5, you can see that the two smaller bedrooms increased about 13 sq. ft. or almost 14% larger and the master bedroom also increased in size. With this three-bedroom example, two small halls use about 9-10 sq. ft. each. The original hall shown in Fig. 5.4 was 48 sq. ft. and was thus reduced to only 18-20 sq. ft. The minor differences in total square footage are due to the wall lengths using space in each version. One more lesson can be drawn from this three bedroom example: A 2-bedroom, 2-bath version would not need the second mini hall. In the simplified master bedroom layout, with the master bath private, the door simply opens into the bedroom. Since no mini hall is needed, this square footage could be added to say, the closet. Again, the more rooms to access, the overhead costs increase. In modest homes one has to be relentless in evaluating any potentially wasted space. There is no space to fritter away.

For balance, consider that any floor plan layout has trade-offs. These floor plans, with the great room in the center, limit the available exterior wall options for windows and doors. However, the layout improves one of the bedrooms to have more windows. In Chapter 12 we will see one enhancement to the centered great room, using a minor bump out that adds window options lost with the center location. A benefit to the great room public space is that the bedrooms are more private at the ends of the house.

In most chalets, which are similar to the New England cape-style home, one bedroom, preferably the master, is on the first floor. Since the owners prefer the master bathroom to be private, you must pass through the master bedroom door to get to this larger bathroom. But, if you have two doors to this bathroom, it is not private. The added second bathroom door has its own design/space issues. The floor plan of this smaller 25' × 40' footprint has only 1,000 sq. ft. of room to work with, meaning the second bedroom must be upstairs. This second bedroom is usually located over the master bedroom. Thus, less privacy results, making it harder for the intended master bedroom to be a "master", compared to the second bedroom. With the second bedroom upstairs, a second bath is needed up there. If the owner wants to keep the master bath private to the owners, a powder room, or half bath, is needed for visitors on the main level. The cost for this extra half bath is about $5,000 — most people won't want to clean an extra bathroom when only two people live in the house. Think of this half bath need as a grenade — it blows up the floor plan. Try to fit it in the floor plan in Figure 12.1 without some pain.

Note in Figure 12.1 that the stairs to the basement are out of the way. Stairs are necessary, of course, but they are not quite a grenade. In the typical mountain Chalet, they are usually in the middle of the 25' × 40' Chalet footprint and have a chopping-up effect. Since this stair zone has to service the loft, or second floor area, as well as the

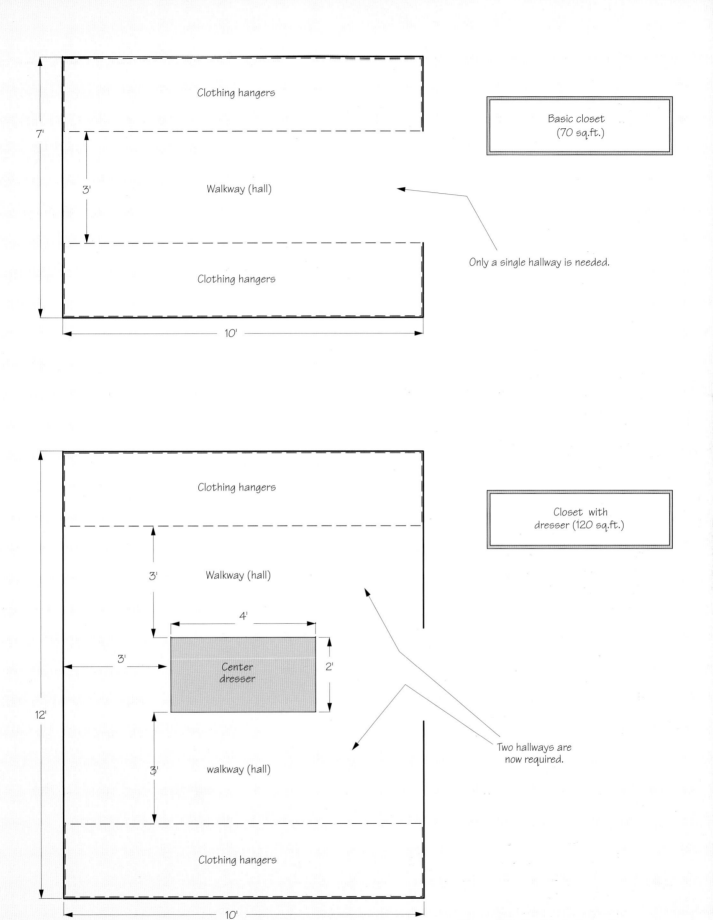

Figure 5.3 Double-hall penalty.

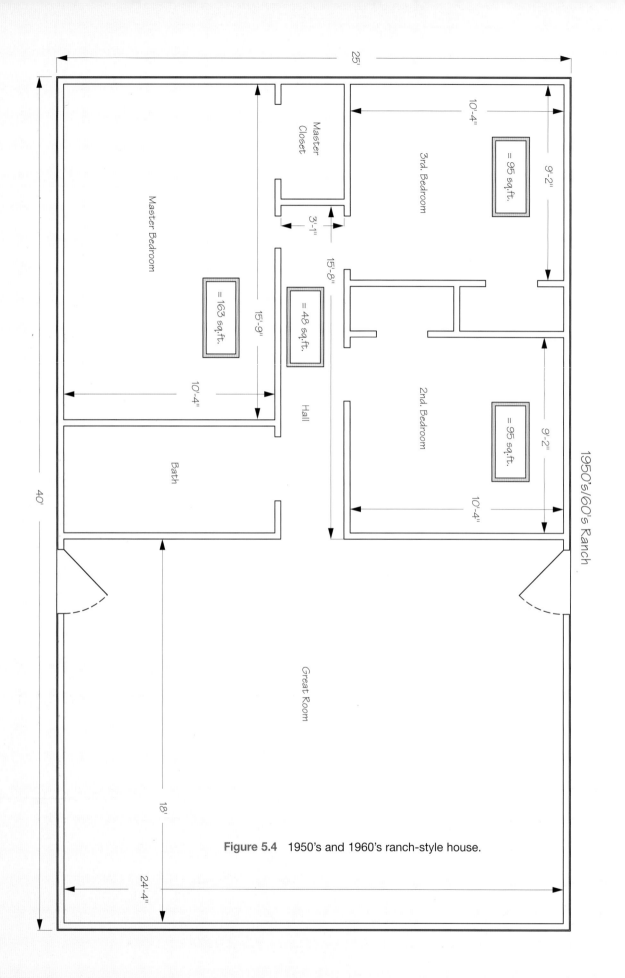

Figure 5.4 1950's and 1960's ranch-style house.

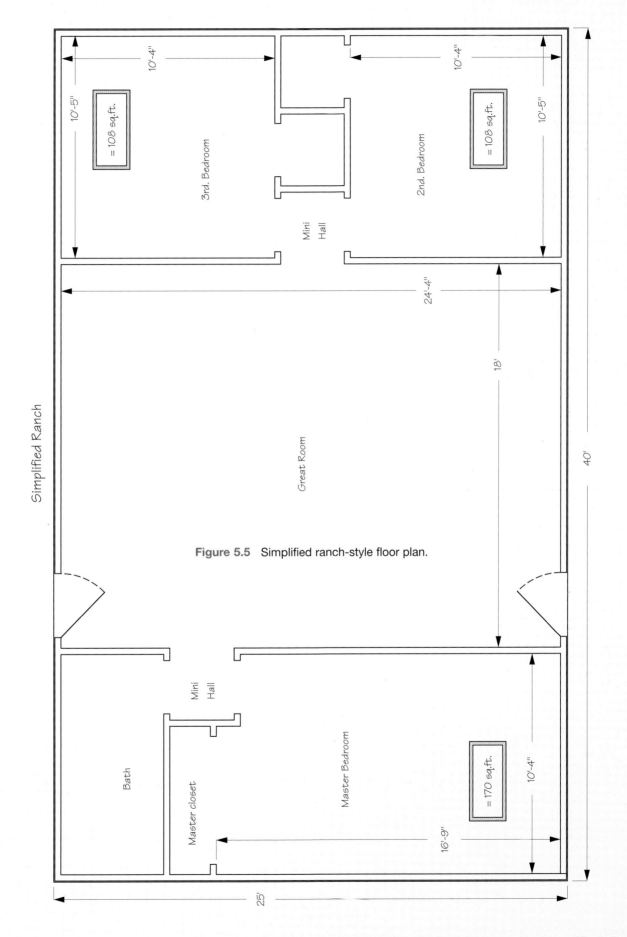

Figure 5.5 Simplified ranch-style floor plan.

basement, all of these zones should line up vertically and require some hallway space overhead. Applying the ranch concept in Figure 12.1, you can see that the matching basement footprint of the 20' by 36' great room area on the main floor (which is open by using Timber Trusses) also nets a potential 20' by 36' future den in the basement. Adding a second floor or loft to Figure 12.1 would require changing the ceiling height (from an 8/12 pitch to a 12/12 pitch).

Figure 5.6 shows the loft-style Timber Truss in the air, being lifted by the boom truck. You can see this trapezoidal shape with the tall 12/12 roof pitch in the center and the shorter knee walls (about 5' high). With this 25'-wide shape, the optimum width of this loft room is only 12'. Refer back to Figure 4.1 and note this loft room area, superimposed inside the 12/12 roof line. This 12/12 pitch, 25'-26'-wide triangle results in an inside ceiling height of about 13' at the ridge peak in the loft and 22'-23' feet from the main floor. This height, in an open space of this size, (the great room), is not as cozy as the second floor loft space that is closer to the ceiling. The cathedral ranch ceiling of 13' to 15' above the floor is a balance of comfort of these two extremes. The owner of the two-story home (Figures 5.6 to 5.8) also noted that when the great room chalet-height ceiling is shared with the second floor, the loft section is not private. Think about stay-over guests — grandkids snuggling up in the loft for sleeping. Any noise in the connected main great room area ruins this use. Thus, a ranch-style home is a good choice. Let's continue to look at our future home's floor plan.

We have located the bedrooms and bathrooms, so let's focus on the great-room area. Most clients desire that this area be "open". A structural and architectural requirement is a vaulted or cathedral-style ceiling. It is sloped like to the outside roof and not flat at 8' high, as in most homes in the 1960s. A reasonably sloped ceiling, say, from 4/12 to 8/12 is a moderate choice. (Structural and low-energy issues are detailed in Chapters 6 and 7.) We have created a *cathedral ranch* for the main floor space, which is the *principal living* space. The basement level, the second priority, would cost less with the resulting flat-ceiling structure.

With this architectural shape defined, you can now develop a range of sizes for the great room. For example, the 720 sq. ft. great room in Figure

12.1 is judged by most visitors as a good size. Most weekend cabins I have seen or designed typically have a 25' by 24' space, (600 sq. ft.) allocated for the great room. Typically, it will be the main gathering place for weekend guests, family weekend-only stay-overs and the central place for holiday visits.

One Christmas, when my daughter was young, our family drove to a central Florida beach location. This was because the patriarch uncle wanted all of his daughters, my wife's cousins, now far-flung with their busy careers, to gather at a single location. His sister, my mother-in-law, had three daughters joining this holiday celebration. Do the math: six cousins, boyfriends, husbands, an extra uncle and aunt and my infant daughter. Remember the high-rise condominiums with the railing-view of the beach I talked about in a previous chapter? We packed everyone in one of those small 2-bedroom, 2-bathroom rental layouts for the gift-exchange gathering. (We had multiple units, but not one larger one.) Think how much better this family gathering would have felt in the great room in Figure 12.1.

The horizontal concept can be applied to installing windows, like the triple-window combination suggested earlier for the master bedroom. These three windows, with about 50 sq. ft., provide a 12'-wide panoramic view. If you selected four, 3-0 by 5-0 traditional double-hung, lower-grade wood windows, you require 60 sq. ft. of window (more cost) to gain the same horizontal viewing area, which is more chopped up. Figure 12.8 shows a three-horizontal-windows look.

According to the USGBC LEED point system for commercial buildings, only the space from 30" off the floor to 7' is counted as the *view* zone. The upper area lets more daylight deeper into the room (like higher clerestory windows) for less energy use during the day. The area below 30" is an energy penalty in commercial and residential buildings.

The same fundamentals apply to garages. The upper cut on sloped terrain will need addressing and have costs. Assume that the builder or property owner desires to be a good steward to the development's specific building guidelines. Also, factor in county and state environmental directives, which address proper handling of this erosion control issue. In Georgia, as in many states, our Soil and Water Conservation Commission requires that all general contractors and/or sub-contractors who cause soil/terrain disturbance need to have someone on their staff certified to the Soil and Water Conservation Commission's standards of operation. A certified person, with their certification card in hand, must be present for the county inspector to conduct inspections. In our own development's architectural codes, not only do we have to structurally stabilize this terrain properly (to prevent erosion, poor water floor control, etc.) but it must be cosmetically similar to the community, for example, rustic. You cannot have bare concrete exposed to view when driving by the home. You must cover this retaining wall surface with stone, stucco or paint. You will likely have a long section in order to take the driveway/transition area out to the access road and not just to the cut.

What do all of these landscaping issues have to do with the horizontal idea? The typical scene in vertical cabins is to have the garage located in the basement, with a garage door on the open, daylight side. This will get us into trouble. First, who is using this garage and what is their typical daily practice? The owner drives up to the house, somewhere in the upper cut zone, to get close to the entry door (typically close to the kitchen) to unload groceries. They almost never get back into the car and park it in the garage below. *Below* is the key word here. The usual height from this "convenient" lower garage location to the main house entry point, or main floor, is 10' to 11'. This translates into about 16 steps from there to the kitchen, using the maximum step-riser code specs. If one attempts to disguise this transition, via creative landscaping ideas (more cost), gravity wins again. People just don't use the garage. In our rural-based, mountain-sloped hotbed of retirees, I rarely see the garage ever occupied by a car. It seems to be the depository of "stuff" and doesn't fit the owner's day-to-day use pattern.

What about the upper terrain cut? This is where the garage should be located, either attached or nearby detached, depending on design tastes. Properly implemented, this uphill garage location achieves some of the retaining wall/landscaping issues. (More on this idea in Chapter 11, combined with yard maintenance). Even our garage can apply both the less-is-more and the horizontal concepts.

Are you ready for one other key benefit? This deals with gravity. Water runs downhill, correct?

The garage location, with proper drainage around the wall and proper erosion-control techniques applied, can assist in water control of the home. You already have much of the uphill water under control prior to getting close to your main living structure. Not only will you have a better garage, you will have a better basement. This action also points to the next interlinking of this garage process. Since you now have both a ranch, horizontal plan and a garage out of the basement zone, the net area left in the basement is space for house expansion needs. The higher cost of the main-level living area and the lower cost of the basement space for future expansion balance each other. The detached garage structure can be simpler and cost less (for example, having 2×4 walls) because it is for a car and not human living. These costs are averaged out. The safety factor and the code related costs of having an auto near a living zone are also compounded by what a leaky garage door does to the building envelope. Also, carbon monoxide from car exhaust leaking into the human living zone is a safety threat. This also works when only a carport budget is available. The use of the structural, erosion-control concrete wall is still beneficial to the carport's structure. There are more costs for having the car go "down" to this basement zone.

An acquaintance of mine was building a retirement home on a large property site and a significant footprint. The mountain site had many of the terrain issues discussed. There was a sub-wall section 10'-12' high and tapering along the long, low side of the building. (Remember that a sub-wall is below the basement level. The house was approaching a square due to the large size.) With a garage at the lower, driveway end of the basement, this subwall appeared to me to need erosion control below it, adding to the cost. My estimate of the upper cut also was that it would be 55'-65' long, with a maximum height of about 8' and tapering down to 6' along this run. For simplicity, let's assume that a cross-tie wall is not correct. An 8"-10'-thick reinforced, concrete retaining wall was needed. Let's say this wall costs about $8,000. Let's also note that the community architectural guidelines require the bare concrete be covered. Using a modest stone cover (veneered; not dry stack, local grade material, reasonable labor rate, etc.) would cost about $4,000. The main costs, not counting drain rock, pipe,

Figure 5.6 Loft trusses being lifted into place at mountain chalet.

related landscaping labor and material, would be about $12,000. If the garage was placed in the upper cut, using about 25' of the 60' wall length — maybe more since there were connecting side wall concrete needs not yet counted — which would be part of the garage structure. In the rock covering, about $1,600 worth of the stone covering would not be needed. If you include another 24' of the connecting sidewall (the garage end wall required fitting the garage to the natural terrain) the rock covering cost is higher. Other cosmetic- influenced decisions compounded things. My conclusion was that better planning would have yielded the client a better, usable solution for not much more, if any, costs.

One variation on the horizontal theme. Some baby-boomer retirement homes will be built in places where a basement is not practical. Popular areas such as Florida and the great plain's states will have this situation. However, using many of the concepts already discussed, plus using technical points in succeeding chapters will be beneficial.

Two recent design efforts should indicate these benefits. The first project was with a group from Florida after the terrible 2004 hurricane season. With South and central Florida recovering from hurricanes Jean and Charlie, some counties had over 10-20% of homes destroyed or beyond repair. One county had lost almost a fourth of their residential units. Their focus was on faster construction and hurricane-resistant structures. Since some of my projects have been quickly erected using SIP wall designs and our Timber Trusses, we began discussions. The strong, double-layer (solid foam sandwiched between 2×6 decking trusses $5/8$"-thick top sheathing) roof system was also of interest. Texas Tech in Lubbock, Texas, has done a lot of testing on wind damage and the structural superiority of SIP's is documented. In fact, I believe that SIP's are approved in the tougher, Florida residential building code. If you check the FLASH.org Web site, relating to safe Florida homes, you can confirm that their minimum wall sheathing is now $5/8$"-thick (this is not the typical code, which is a minimum $7/16$"-thick OSB, for example). Just prior to this hurricane application, I had been developing a line of floor plans for a *kit* concept targeted for

Figure 5.7 Loft trusses prior to the 2×4 T&G paneling.

Figure 5.8 Loft decking partially installed.

South Georgia hunting plantations for use as rentals for hunter clients. Both sites are low, flat terrain where no basement would exist and building on a slab base is the norm. As the projects moved forward, the base unit was the Chalet, 1½- to 2-story building shape. (Refer to Figures 5.6 - 5.8 of the loft truss.) These locations were higher density building areas, so using a second floor to keep the footprint smaller was a key requirement. However, in Florida, the normal architecture is low-profile roofs, typically hipped, for better hurricane resistance, while using normal stick framing. Using the timber approach, particularly using the heavy loft Timber Trusses and the 2×6 tongue-and-groove (T&G) decking on both the knee walls and the floor decking, nailed directly on the trusses, is incredibly strong. Complete bridging throughout the entire house strengthens tall, gable-end walls at the weak hinge point at the top of the main floor wall. Despite this not being a good fit for their market, some interesting floor-plan concepts did result. The most significant factor was, if you were to use this loft concept, it only worked efficiently if you used it *completely in the entire second floor*. Thus, you use all loft trusses and don't use the decorative open ceiling, which requires using a Queen Truss for example, in the great room zone. For a 25'×40' footprint, you can obtain almost 1500 sq. ft. of space. You could then have two medium-size bedrooms in the loft area and a bath with the master bedroom being on the main level. Since the construction was on a slab, finding the utility zones for HVAC mechanical, ducting and electrical runs was difficult. The little triangle corners of the Loft Truss were perfect for the utilities as well as closet space. Space efficiency at its best. The conclusion of this southern hurricane project is that the resulting floor plan was similar to the New England Capes.

The above spatial design could be built with pre-engineered wood trusses and minimal framing strength, if costs become an issue. Most of these higher-cost techniques will average out over the life of the house.

The less-is-more and go-horizontal rules can be used to make building decisions that will save money and make a more efficient house.

06

Low Energy = Daughter's College Tuition

Our family's tale of our earlier North Atlanta home (20-plus years) demonstrates how important the time factor of low-energy use is to family finances.  The monthly energy savings from this home was approximately what we saved for our daughter's college fund. One of our friends frequently reminds me, chuckling, with this phrase: "Small bedroom and a college fund". This story parallels many of the baby-boomer trends. Our family made a life-changing downsizing decision before our retirement years. We moved to our mountain cabin about eight years earlier than planned. We had designed and built the cabin using a lot of the concepts discussed to this point and also many more explained later. My daughter's new bedroom was smaller than her bedroom in the Atlanta suburban home we were leaving. As these discussions evolved, I told my daughter she surely could have a larger bedroom in the cabin, or a smaller bedroom and a college fund!

This was not just a father/daughter teasing game. I had a monthly savings plan, in stocks, during most of our time in the earlier home based on the difference of our actual energy costs and the energy costs for a typical neighborhood home. Our utility bills, totally electric, were around $55/month in the early 1980s. By 2001, when we were selling this home to move into the mountain cabin, I would tell potential buyers that our electric bills were in the "low eighties" per month. Because of the disbelieving look of buyers and realtors and also desiring to audit her husband, my wife totaled the previous twelve month's utility costs and the monthly average was $83! Thus, we were putting about $75/month into our daughter's college savings plan, saved from the difference of the average utility bill at that time.

The monthly usage of kilowatt hours did not increase significantly. The 51% increase from this period was just the normal increase of energy costs. Prospective buyers were telling us their own energy sob stories as they viewed our home, which fueled their doubts. Buyers told us were paying $200-$400/month for their utilities in small condominiums or homes with the same floor plan as ours.

Before outlining some of the technical aspects of our suburban Atlanta home, please look at the picture of the house in figure 6.1. Due to the large lot and distance to the main road, this photo was taken more than halfway up the driveway. Things are frequently hidden in homes.

PASSIVE SOLAR ENERGY

The primary revelation is that this is a passive-solar home. The long, wide side you see is the South-facing wall with most of the windows located on this wall. (See Chapter 9 for more information about windows on a South-facing wall.) This was inspired by the mid-1970's energy crisis. I was interested in energy-efficient design in my early engineering career. In 1980, before I designed this home, I took an energy-efficient home-design course in the architecture department of an Atlanta-area university, Southern Poly Tech. This course, and the inspi-

ration of Edward Mazria's landmark book, *The Passive Solar Energy Book,* by Rodale Press, set me toward the goal of designing energy-efficient homes. From Fig. 6.1, (or from the curb) can you tell that it is passive-solar?

The technical challenge is that it is a *bermed* house. No, not a weird solar cave. The lower back and west-side walls are below grade. 1,200 sq. ft. of the main level is bermed while the upper 700 sq. ft. is above grade. The master bedroom suite and a small office occupy the upper level. The lower level could fall under appraisal guidelines as a finished basement. However, this berm, in home plans, could also be the called the terrace level. The design challenge, as other designers and architects who specialize in this area attest, is getting the flow of this design to be like other houses.

The concept is valid, but design issues like high-grade foundation waterproofing and good exterior insulation of the concrete mass are two essential design elements that need to be addressed.

I used a wood exterior; specifically cedar siding. This decision is typical if you are controlling the building process. Despite the desire to use more masonry on the exterior, my budget would not allow it. Wish I had though. Several stain jobs were required while we lived there. By the way, did you know that Atlanta-based woodpeckers like to practice on cedar siding as the weather turns colder? I learn that the hard way. Being a pioneer sometimes hurts.

Note the shape and appearance of the main house and the attached garage. The house is a *clerestory*-style roof. There are two different roofs with an upper gap between the front and back roofs, which accommodates the higher clerestory windows. The garage is a wedge shape, which is also suited for passive solar. The clerestory shape is fairly common, while the wedge is more radical. The basic house shape is not much different from most houses prior to when the "six-foot roof rule" invaded American suburbia.

Building techniques used in 1980 were 2×6 stud exterior walls with both foam and thick fiberglass

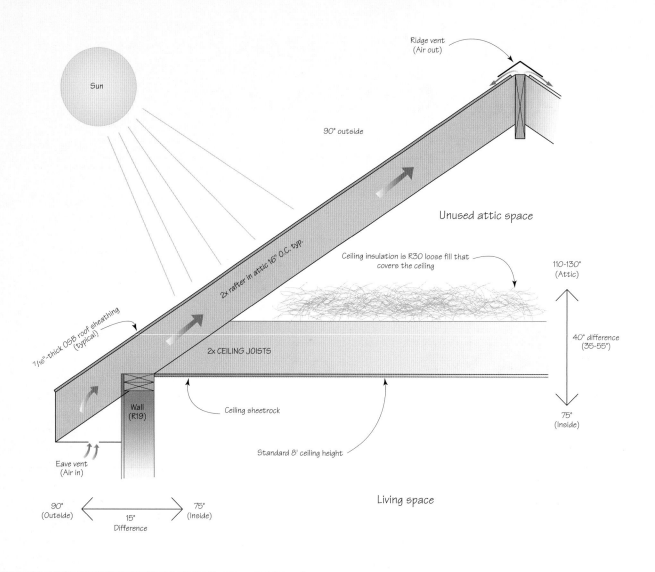

Figure 6.2 Conventional-framed "vented" roof.

insulation — considered radical. (Radical enough to help put my daughter through college.) Another technique was to use a non-vented roof design. This means that the roof insulation was a solid-foam product sandwiched between two sheathing layers on top of the structural members. I did not have exterior air flowing up into an unused attic space. I used this vaulted space and utilized better insulation than normal. The structural members were 4×6, rustic, exposed beams. This was a cathedral ranch-style in the roof areas that had this vaulted design. This non-vented roof is now accepted in the building code, (but considered expensive as one trainer noted in a code update class) but it was radical at the time. We enjoyed comfort using the roof design despite the fact that the bank draw sheet also told me it was too expensive. Asphalt

shingle life wasn't any different than our long-time neighbor's. This real-world testing was three times longer than the average American family lives in one home.

A few years after construction, an attached greenhouse/solarium was added in front of the great room area. This was a nice addition to the home that I will detail in Chapter 9. Think of it as an alternative to a screened-in porch.

I will outline some energy saving techniques that I now recommend. Some people think "A house needs to breathe". I say houses don't breathe, they leak.

Here's a list of my "informal" building guidelines. Building codes vary a lot in the United States. These are mid-values. For example, in Wisconsin or Northern Vermont, they need to be increased.

INFORMAL GUIDELINES

Roof Design:
- Non-vented, solid-foam filled
- Minimum R30, approaching R40 insulating value
- Caulked and sealed design
- Top cover is W.R.Grace ICE/Watershield on entire roof
- Heavier Timber Frame/Truss or SIP style structure

Wall Design:
- 2×6 stud exterior framing, if conventional, with foam-filed cavity insulation, either open- or closed-cell foam
- Minimum R19, approaching R25 insulating value
- ⅝"-thick exterior sheathing, particular in windy zones
- Normal 16" spacing on studs
- Insulated structural headers over doors & windows
- Insulated framing T's if facing exterior of building
- Exterior air barrier on exterior (Tyvek)
- Consider ICE/Water shield on lower 30" if moist-climate issue or SIP walls (Structural Insulated Panels)
- 6" panels if using EPS foam (about R24) or 4" panels if foam is higher R-value/inch
- Ice/Water Shield on lower 30" exterior

Windows Design:
- Best one can afford — minimum is low maintenance exterior (aluminum or vinyl-clad as first choices)
- Double-pane insulated, LOW-E, possibly argon filled
- EnergyStar rated as general guide
- U about .33 (R then is about R3)
- Solar Heat Gain, SHGC, about .40 max
- Tight-sealing design like casements, not sliding or double-hung

Basement Foundation Wall Design:
- Poured reinforced concrete, thickness per local safe design guidance (8-10" thickness typical)
- Exterior waterproofing should be flexible, non-hardening like Tuff-n-Dri
- Exterior insulation should be R5 to R10, like Tuff-n-Dri (note outside)
- Thermal break on slab wherever possible (EnergyEdgeForm)
- Radon vent pipe from below basement slab floor to roof!

Floor Design:
- Assume the will be a basement version included in the building envelope, floor insulation not needed but possibly desired for sound damping
- Use engineered floor trusses (18"-24" high)
- Radiant heating

HVAC Design:
- High-efficiency heat pumps in more temperate zones
- Dual-fuel backup heat-pump in colder climates
- Possibly geo-thermal heat pumps
- Radiant floor heating if practical details can be solved
- Integrate fresh air intake, simple vent or ERV/HRV
- Stove/Fireplace auxiliary heat – direct vent air intake to combustion only, no vent-free, seal the viewing door

Hot Water Heating:
- Tank-less if gas source
- Hi-efficiency if electric (Marathon)
- Tank-less partial local boost if total-electric home
- Consider active solar water heating panels

Lighting:
- EnergyStar rated as a starting point
- CFL types when dimming not issue
- Consider emerging LED technology for spot locations

ROOF DETAILS

First I want to address the roof design that is so critical, assuming the general building envelope design is good for the overall energy-use picture. If you look at the HVAC contractor's normal guides, like their "J" manual, and study both manual heat load calculations and also the RESCHECK, United

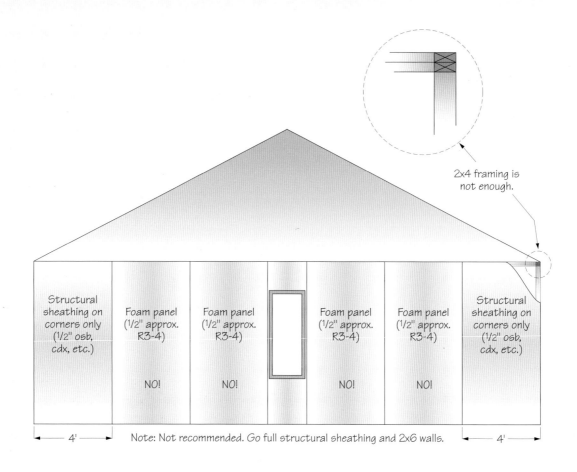

2x4 framing is
not enough.

Structural
sheathing on
corners only
(1/2" osb,
cdx, etc.)

Foam panel
(1/2" approx.
R3-4)

Foam panel
(1/2" approx.
R3-4)

Foam panel
(1/2" approx.
R3-4)

Foam panel
(1/2" approx.
R3-4)

Structural
sheathing on
corners only
(1/2" osb,
cdx, etc.)

NO!   NO!   NO!   NO!

|← 4' →| Note: Not recommended. Go full structural sheathing and 2x6 walls. |← 4' →|

Figure 6.3 2×4 wall with foam sheathing. NO!

States Energy endorsed software, the magnitude of energy loss or heat gain (summer in the south) is the largest. Air infiltration loss is important. I am rigid in using a *non-vented* roof design — regardless of the roofing material used. I also believe that the typically stronger structure of either pre-made SIPs or my regionally-preferred Timber Style roofs is a beautiful example of where the "code is the minimum" bites you. We have many examples, even in North Georgia, where hurricanes, tornadoes, or simply high winds have caused serious injury. Hurricane Opal, in 1995, despite both Atlanta and the North Georgia mountains, over 300 to 400 miles from landfall, still show the scars of fallen trees. I know of one weekend cabin in the North Georgia cabins, still in framing, that was destroyed by one of Opal's felled trees. A spring 1998 tornado zipped through the North Atlanta suburbs and felled about 100,000 trees in Gwinnett County alone. Texas Tech's testing will show you the potential of all of these wind-born natural wood missiles. My neighbor's home, hundreds of feet outside of

this 1998 tornado direct path, had a 3" pine limb through his roof. Fortunately no injuries resulted. Many injuries were due to roofs built only to the code. These are not just a few scares, they are real and happen more often than one realizes. Note that any money invested (6' roof rule) for appearance would not have helped in these situations. And yes, there was a dormer or two blown off by the 1998 tornado in my neighborhood! My recommendations are founded in investing in quality structure, first and foremost.

Not only is the sandwich style, non-vented, two-layer roof stronger, for the above safety reasons, it is more resistant to air infiltration than a vented roof. Think how a vented roof works, particularly in the warmer summer periods. Figure 6.2 shows some basics of this traditional roof framing. Let's assume it is a 90° day. My experience, even north of Florida's hot and humid extremes, the average temperature in a vented roof is easily 110-120°. You would be shocked at how many hit 130° or more! If you have this large volume of hot, humid air, your ceiling insulation (likely R19 –R30 fiberglass or loose fill style) on the flat, typically sheetrock ceiling is working against a temperature differential of about 40° — assuming you want 75° inside your living space and the temperature in the attic is 115°. (Note that the "lovely", steep-pitched roof with the six-foot-rule appearance has significantly more volume of this hot humid air than your parent's little ranch roof.) With my suggested approach, the vaulted, non-vented, solid-foam-paneled, tightly-sealed roof R31 (better product!) is working against only a 15° differential (90° less 75°). Looking ahead at Figure 7.1, note the main components of one type of a non-vented roof structure. Now, tell me again how the other vented, big air filed roof is better? It's not better, it's simply cheaper — or is it? A few-to-several dollars more per square foot is the real cost, plus whatever extra structural design element's costs (fancier wood, beam size, finish, etc.) you prefer. The important summary of this typical vented roof structure is that between your head and the outside world is only $7/16$"-thick OSB and $1/2$"-thick sheetrock. Is this what you desire protecting you in a last home? Think about the interrelated costs of the typical roof's excess cosmetic features with this new information about real quality.

Add to this that Georgia–Pacific's recent marketing of mould-resistant sheetrock, targeted at these flat and the more decorative "tray" ceilings. Think about hot, moist air condensing on these flat "vented" ceilings if the dew point is right. I believe that both the larger temperature differential plus these physically larger attic zones, coupled with the need for tighter homes increases this problem measurably. By the way, the popular "tray ceiling" is just more of the same, no real improvement in the ceiling structure or insulating value, just money spent only on "look". This reminds me of another trendy thing — the focus on *faux* finishes. We have fauxed-this and fauxed-that so much that we now have a "false" ceiling. (Well, maybe not false, but not really that good either, in my opinion!) There is apparently a huge market for this cheaper ceiling design since it "looks so good".

Diligence is mandatory for sealing up all possible areas of air infiltration. A last step is to cover the entire outer-roof sheathing with a quality, self-adhering product like WR Grace ICE/WaterShield. This product is now a common building code requirement in New England and other snow belts due to ice damming, which creates water under roofing shingles for the first few feet of the roof eave's edge. I say do the entire roof. The cost is around a dollar per square foot — less than 1 percent of the total house's cost — over builder-grade tar paper is pretty cheap insurance for me. As a reality check, gaze upward toward the sky tonight and see what portion of the house structure is protecting most of your largest investment!

WALL DETAILS

For the wall design, my favorite is SIP modules, whenever it can be implemented. We frequently use conventional 2×6 framing (with some panelization), coupled with spray-foam insulation after framing and before finishing the interior, in more complex designs not easily serviced by SIPs. Briefly, the spray-foam insulation process yields a huge benefit by insuring that the entire wall structure is well-sealed against air infiltration. I believe that it also minimizes condensation problems in most environments since it improves the dew point temperature (condensation point) over any insulation technique that allows humid air to get into the condensation point in the first place. The range of costs of both high- and low-density spray-foam is about a dollar or two per square foot more than the typical construction budget for wall insulation. Yes, this will be more than the typical bank-draw line-item figure. But, whose walls do you want well insulated?

A wealth of information on SIPs can be found in *Building with Structural Insulated Panels* by Michael Morley (Taunton Press). Basically, SIPs have several advantages I have already discussed. Not only are they very energy efficient (higher R-Values), they inherently have better sealing qualities (less air infiltration), usually erect faster and can lead to more module-sized home designs. At more than one of our projects, using first-time crews with minimal pre-training, all of the main floor walls were erected in one day. We worked with only the smaller 4'×8' panels, pre-framed window and gable-end wall sections, and we did not need a boom truck for the first day. For one project we even used larger 8'-tall by 16'-wide panels (at the end of the bedroom module) without a boom truck. The second day, the gable ends and Timber Trusses were lifted in place with a boom truck. The real value of this technology is not just the energy savings, but the value of the resulting wall strength and less labor to erect. It is now well-documented how strong these homes are in high-wind situations, including extreme events such as tornadoes and hurricanes. The most significant potential of SIPs is that it shows promise as a good building-block approach towards more efficient residential building. (See Chapter 8.)

Let's look at typical 2×4 wall construction techniques that meet the code (minimum) but have serious penalties later. Remember that this approach is trying to "save money". (Remember? We "need" this wasted money to spend on all the "essential" Arts-&-Crafts trim details.) The technical point is that the building code only requires plywood or OSB exterior sheathing at the building corners, for bracing the structure, say, for wind resistance. With emphasis finally moving into the energy sections of the building code, more insulation is required in the walls. This type of compromise resulted: Some builders simply used the minimum ½"-thick structural sheathing (it is typically ⁷/₁₆"-thick) at these few points and filled in the intermediate points with a ½"-thick, foam, continuous panel insulation. This R3-to-R4 foam paneling does improve the overall wall R-value

somewhat, since the stronger structural sheathing values at the corners is only about R0.5, as shown in Figure 6.3. I can't tell you how many of these alleged Arts-&-Crafts-style homes, in many regions, have this structural compromise! But, it meets the code, doesn't it?

Are you now suspicious of 2×4-stud-wall construction? Many buyers of homes never realize that these walls are in their huge purchase. It's just "details" that are covered up when you are touring the finished house. In 2006, in a suburban county north of Atlanta, a 105 mile-per-hour wind microburst hit a neighborhood of homes. The three homes in the newspaper photo simply gave-in and failed against this amount of wind (which is only 25 percent above code). The siding and trim missing on these homes clearly showed this "cost-saving" approach in action. At a builder's meeting years earlier, I stressed that this design approach was marginal. The *increased cost* was immediately offered to counter to my point that better quality is needed.

There is more. Within a few months of this wind and the ensuing home failures, a hot news story in the Atlanta area was based upon this wonderful "savings" approach to building homes. An Atlanta gang was arrested for break-ins and robbing of homes targeted with this style construction. They

Figure 6.4 Insulated headers and T's in the shop.

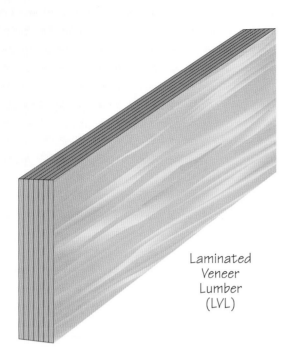

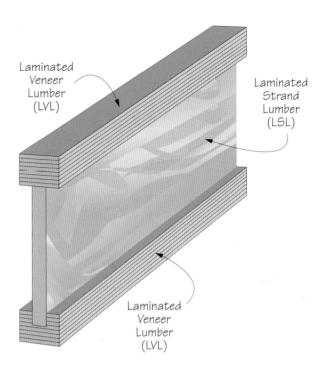

Figure 6.5 Laminated Veneer Lumber (LVL)

Figure 6.6 I-joist made of Laminated Strand Lumber (LSL) and Laminated Veneer Lumber (LVL).

simply used a utility knife to cut through the vinyl siding, through the foam panel and quietly entered the homes during daylight hours. They did not even need to break windows, which would have been noisy! This window-breaking scenario was also offered as a counter-argument at the builder's meeting. One may be resigned to have this cheaper wall structure, due to budget constraints, in your first home during your younger, transient, career years. But, our focus here is on a more permanent home. I say save money using 2×6-stud exterior walls and full-structural sheathing — then fully insulating with a superior product like spray foam!

WINDOW DETAILS

The window decision process is the next area for potential improvement. For example, a 60'-wide by 8'-high wall, located on the south side of a house, has several windows. There is 150 sq. ft. of glass area in three, triple-window sets. With a good quality window, the insulation value is about R3, while the main wall is about R19 (if built to the minimum code). This means the average of the wall is about R14. If the structural headers over windows and wall T's (about R1) are not insulated and have

air leaks, the effective R value drops below, say, R10. An R10 wall loses about 10% of the energy, an R20 loses about 5%, an R30 loses about 3%, etc. More windows means more insulation is required.

In Chapter 9 we will see how good this South wall window choice was compared to the North wall. It gets worse. Older windows on a 2×4 wall, are about R1 to 1.5. Get the best windows you can afford. If your builder commits to coming by your new home monthly to subsidize your energy costs, then you can use inexpensive windows. Oh, he did not come by with a check in hand?

Another factor in choosing windows is to keep the shapes simple. The curved, round, octagon or hexagons all have more costs to bear than just the shape. The framing, exterior finish, exterior trim, interior finish and interior trim will increase the costs. And sealing these windows against energy loss and water infiltration is more difficult. Since you might have a trapezoid shape in the gable areas, you can use this complex shape to increase cosmetic appeal. Another area of enhancing cosmetic treatment is in your choice of entry-door windows. A high-quality door is already designed to solve the problems of a complex shaped window.

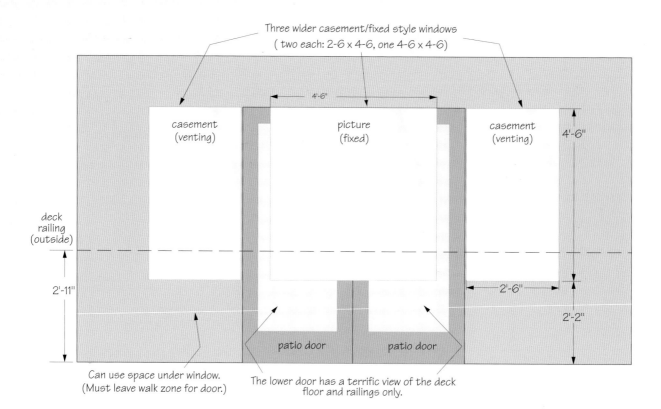

Three wider casement/fixed style windows
(two each: 2-6 x 4-6, one 4-6 x 4-6)

casement
(venting)

4'-6"

picture
(fixed)

casement
(venting)

4'-6"

deck
railing
(outside)

2'-11"

2'-6"

2'-2"

patio door

patio door

Can use space under window.
(Must leave walk zone for door.)

The lower door has a terrific view of the deck
floor and railings only.

Figure 6.7   Three windows vs french doors.

So a fancier glass shape, say an oval, already in the door, is a smart choice to gain visual appeal.

DOORS VS. WINDOWS

Another design choice is the trade off between doors and windows. Figure 6.4 shows the differences. It is tempting for a homeowner to prefer a door that opens to the deck or patio. Typically they desire a French-door style as seen in magazines and plan books. Before you choose this, consider a few things. First, odds are you will rarely use this door, but you will know it is there in the winter months. Second, even the highest-quality doors are more susceptible to leaking (air or rain) than the same quality level of windows. Third, for air ventilation purposes, a door is not the same as a window (will you crack it to let fresh air in?). Fourth, a window and a door have different traffic flow and using them will affect how you use the floor space around them (can you put a small table in front of a French door?). And finally, a high-quality, clad-aluminum, low-maintenance, French patio door for this application will cost about $1,100-$1,500. The recommended three-window technique shown

in Figure 6.7, discussed in the Go Horizontal section in Chapter 5, will be at the lower end of this price range, for the same quality product. Note the improvement in the view out the glass section of the doors closer to the ground, not at natural eye view where the windows focus lies. Guess which configuration you will really enjoy years from now?

Now that we have selected good-quality windows and doors, we need to properly install them. There are many detailed window guides in the market as well as the window manufacturer's included instructions. The two key focus areas are properly sealing the exterior nailing flanges and the gap inside between the window frame and the rough window framing (typically about a $1/4$" gap). For the exterior nailing flanges, we prefer a self-adhesive tape/membrane, like ICE/Water shield or a specifically designed-to-width product that laps over the exterior flanges to the moisture barrier. Most window vendors recommend using a high-grade caulk under the flange and the building face also. Lower-rate expansion foams will fill this small, but leaky, gap on the inside. We don't want the house to "breathe" in this little gap.

STRUCTURAL HEADERS

Our final window/door topic is the structural headers above their rough openings in the framing. Typically, these are built with standard 2× framing wood. For a 2×4 wall, this resulting $1/2"$ gap (two $1\frac{1}{2}"$ widths) is filled with a $1/2"$ plywood spacer or left as an air gap. With the thicker 2×6 wall, the header gap now is $2\frac{1}{2}"$ ($5\frac{1}{2}"$ minus the 3" of framing thicknesses). Since these header areas are major air infiltration zones, they "water down" the effective wall R-value. Improvement in design is needed (R3 vs. R19 insulation value for a 2×6 wall).

I recommend filling this gap with insulation foam pieces as shown in Figure 6.4. The header modules being pre-built in the shop show the white EPS foam filling the gap between the two structural 2×s. The corner T's have the same EPS gap-filling. The EPS is the same product used in SIPs (Structural Insulated Panels discussed in Chapter 8). We have the hot-wire tools for foam cutting and our SIP supplier will pre-cut basic blank sizes, so final cutting is relatively simple. The foam size is fairly accurate, so the final nailing of these modules is improved. We prefer to build the modules using

Figure 6.8 External insulation on foundation.

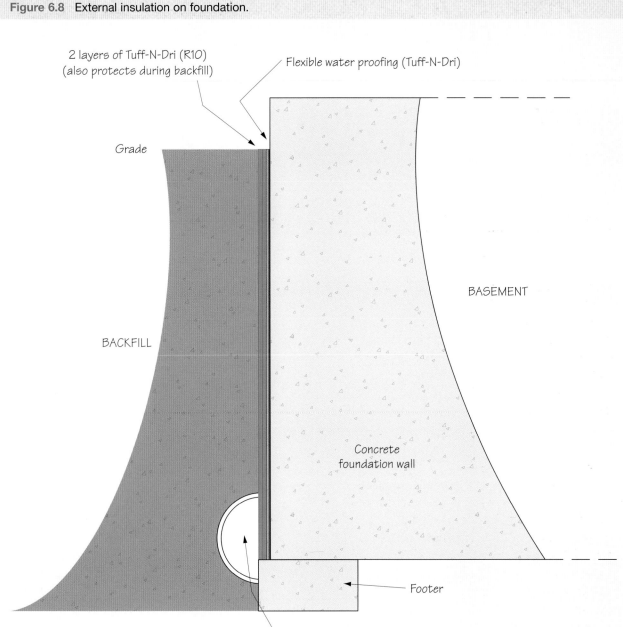

2 layers of Tuff-N-Dri (R10)
(also protects during backfill)

Flexible water proofing (Tuff-N-Dri)

Grade

BASEMENT

BACKFILL

Concrete
foundation wall

Proper gravel and drainage pipe per code

Figure 6.9 Exposed basement slab edge

newer products (see Figs. 6.5 and 6.6) such as LVLs (Laminated Veneer Lumber) and LSLs (Laminated Strand Lumber) in place of these structural 2× pieces. The normal 2× framing will shrink in the wall over time and open up small gaps, where these more stable products will not. Note again that the stable EPS foam improves the air infiltration method even with the normal 2× framing member shrinkage. There are also pre-built, pre-insulated header modules on the market for consideration.

BASEMENT INSULATION

Moving along this low-energy-use path, I'll address basement insulation. The importance of a good basement energy strategy was important in our earlier Atlanta home.

A large portion of our earlier house was the "dreaded" basement. This area's importance is that it is our future expansion space. Finishing a basement is not new — almost everyone knows what a finished basement looks like. (Sort of an American right of suburban evolution.) However, the same construction problems are here and even more prevalent. Frequently, leaky or damp basements are more the norm than ones with good-quality living space. Thus the basement expectation level is set low. One contractor told me that most clients don't even consider this as good space due to typical low quality.

The diligent limiting of the main floor plan to a two-bed, two-bath layout leads to optimizing the basement. If you let the main floor grow to three bedrooms, the budget for the basement will be decreased and will result in using cheap insulation and waterproofing.

In The EnergyStar Model Home detailed in Chapter 12, we will show how averaging the cost of these two floors works. We will not ignore making the basement a quality space. I suggest using R11 for sub-grade basement walls as required by the

Figure 6.10   EnergyEdge-form example on slab edge.

EnergyStar guidelines as a starting point. In some southern climates a minimum of R5 is required by code. I stress putting insulation on the outside of the foundation, not inside. This will hold the thermal mass of a poured concrete wall (not cinder block) that we have already paid for. How this works is two fold: First, the insulation, even as low as R5 or R10, is working against an average earth temperature of around 58° (except in very cold climates). This benefit drops off the closer you get to the grade level. If you desire your room temperature to be 70°, the differential you have to work against is only 12°. (This is similar to the non-vented roof scenario.) The second factor is that heat movement through concrete is slow. This means speed, not insulating value. The real R thermal value of a concrete wall is only R1. The coupling of even a modest R value insulation, between the concrete and the earth's stable temperature, causes the thermal mass to stay inside the envelope. This

thermal mass concept is the cornerstone of the log home industries thermal-efficiency marketing. It is a valid point by itself, but is made better by insulating the basement.

In Southern climates, building code usually does not allow the use of foam plastic insulation below grade or even several inches above grade due to it possibly being a convenient path for termites. Even the safer borate-treated EPS foam is not allowed. I recommend the Tuff-n-Dri process, which uses two layers of a dense, safe fiberglass-derivative product on the outside wall, over a matching high-grade Tuff-n-Dri waterproofing. This yields R10 over the areas covered. This step also protects the foundation wall waterproof coating from being scratched by rocks during backfilling and packing (see Figure 6.8). Do you perceive another linked-benefit emerging here? For about another dollar/sq. ft. for bermed, wall foundation portions, you have more waterproofing insurance.

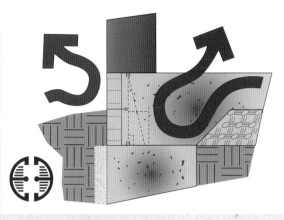

Figure 6.11 EnergyEdge-form energy flow comparison

Another challenging area for the basement, particularly with the foam panel limitation, is the edge of the basement slab. This edge of the slab is exposed on the daylight side of the basement, which slowly leaks off energy. This concrete slab edge feels cooler on the feet near the outer walls. We are evaluating a new product called EnergyEdgeForm that shows some promise for this problem, so, for slab-based structures, this could be a plus.

An otherwise energy-efficient home will demonstrate this tricky problem. Figure 6.9 shows the daylight basement framing section of this house. This Library House home is a larger version (over 2,000 sq. ft.) of the Walnut Mountain EnergyStar home detailed in Chapter 12. The owner could have had this home Energystar certified if they desired to formally validate this structure. It had the same 2×6 exterior wall framing, a similar spray foam exterior R19 wall insulation product and the identical Timber Truss roof structure with the approximate R34 solid foam panel, non-vented roof. The main difference is, due to the less sloping site, the basement had more "daylight" space. That is, the left and right narrow sides of the basement level were above grade, not bermed as shown in the long downhill side in Figure 6.9. Thus, the concrete walls did not "wrap around" these short left and right sides of the basement, which leaves more exposed concrete slab floor edge, like the long daylight side shown.

Let's add some numerical value to this linear distance around this home to help understand this potential energy loss zone. The total perimeter distance of the basement walls (which is the same as the main floor) is about 222'. The portion of the basement with an exposed, non-insulated slab edge is about 153', or over two-thirds of the footprint's perimeter. This good-news/bad-news trade-off simply means that this otherwise superb home will have a basement floor that feels much cooler in winter. This scenario may be acceptable for some clients in our medium-level North Georgia winter climate, but as we go further north in the USA, the issue's significance increases dramatically.

One additional example, almost at press time, demonstrates this slab-edge energy loss with a contrast of the anticipated use of the basement space. In general, as noted in our now established main-floor/main-bedroom strategy and again demonstrated in the 2000 sq. ft. library house, the basement is the future guest space, not the principal owner's bedroom zone. This current project guest house has flipped the typical requirement since the only bedroom is in the basement. This little 24'-wide by 21$\frac{1}{2}$'-deep cabin's key function is that the main floor is a studio. Simply put, it is a great room social area with only three Timber Trusses, a small kitchenette wall, a medium-size bathroom and the staircase zone to get to the basement. The only bedroom, for occasional guests, and a bathroom, occupy the full basement footprint. As noted by the client, the general coolness anticipated in this basement bedroom configuration heightened the desire to improve the temperature climate. Ironically, a

Figure 6.12 EnergyEdge-form concrete slab pouring.

similar terrain, lower-slope issue, like the library house, left only the rear 24'-long backfill wall as a full-height concrete foundation wall. Therefore, almost three-fourths of the perimeter footprint will have this exposed slab-edge heat-loss problem.

We plan to evaluate the EnergyEdge form product for the little guest house. In Figure 6.10, the manufacturer provided a photo similar to our library house basement-slab photo. The gray color in the Energy-Edge picture is the plastic exterior product protecting the encapsulated foam thermal barrier inside. The thermal-break foam is not exposed, which should stop our friendly southern termite friends from finding an easy route into the home.

Figure 6.11 shows a good depiction of energy flow (loss out of) in a typical slab installation and then with the thermal edging included. Note that the southern states do not want us to include the below-slab insulation shown in Figure 6.11. This means we are challenged to find a good energy-efficient solution for concrete slab construction. Figure 6.12 shows the pouring of a concrete slab with the installed edging.

When this basement space is finished later, extra insulating enhancements can be added in the internal walls. This added step is significant for northern climates. Remember that the exposed, above-grade, non-concrete walls mimic the main floor wall strategies.

Let's discuss the *main-floor* energy issues. If we have applied some of our learning at this stage, the floor issues should be much simpler. We have kept the house design clean and all of the main floor is within the building envelope and does not necessarily need insulation between the main floor and the terrace/basement. Some may want to add insulation as a sound barrier, and possibly radiant-heat floors, which will be covered later.

By not keeping things simple, they become complex and require difficult solutions, for example, a *partially-attached* dining room (or other room). I call these partially-attached because they are similar to a screened porch, where they bump out from the exterior of a main section of the house. A key clue is that the underside of this structure is up in the air and not within a simpler building envelope,

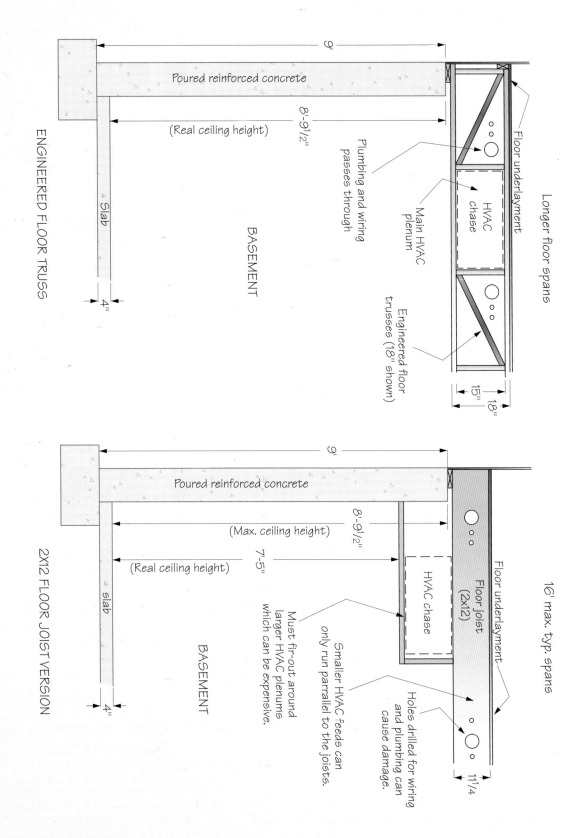

Figure 6.13 Floor trusses vs. 2× joists.

Figure 6.14 HVAC chase in floor trusses.

similar to a crawl space. The significant factor is that this bumped-out room is a conditioned, heated and cooled space. Thus, the floor is an exposed part of the building envelope, and will require a more complex solution. This floor has similar issues as vented roofs except that it is below. Although it does not have the hotter, vented roof temperature, it has the same thermodynamic realities. That is, condensation can occur in this floor zone and cause all those related problems of moisture on structural elements. The most telling symptom relates to comfort. With the typical "cost-effective" insulation solutions usually employed, these rooms have downright cold floors in winter months. I have stayed in several, know builders and acquaintances who have owned them, and they all confirm this discomfort. Just utilize KISS and avoid it altogether with a simpler overall building envelope.

FLOOR TRUSSES

Floor structure guidelines can facilitate some of the thermal issues noted earlier. My first suggestion for your main floor structure is to use engineered floor trusses (see Figure 6.16). Typically, they are 16" to 24" high, and are located on 16" centers, depend-

ing on span and loading. A quality truss vendor's software will engineer these different needs as part of their service.

The minimum of 18" is a practical height, which leaves a 15" gap (minus two flat 2×4s equals 3" less) that most HVAC installations can work with (see Figures 6.14 and 6.15). On larger homes, taller trusses will please your HVAC sub-contractor.

Some builders will tell you how much you can "save" by using 2×10/12 joists. (You may suspect some interlinked costs.) Engineered trusses cost more than standard lumber joists, but you must have adequate room for your utilities: wiring, plumbing and especially the HVAC's larger plenums. Part of the needed space is achieved by hacking into these lower-cost standard lumber joists. I strongly suggest avoiding this approach because the joists will lose structural integrity. If you have a well-designed basement space, and have invested in a taller, stronger, poured concrete foundation wall already for more basement headroom, do you desire to eat up this headroom gain by dropping the larger plenums below the lower-cost joists? (See Figure 6.13.) With lumber joists, if you want to use this space now occupied by the HVAC plenums

Figure 6.15 HVAC installed in floor trusses.

or other runs, you must add furring strips around them. As a result, extra costs are incurred to finish out this ceiling area, rather than being able to use the floor-truss bottoms. My analysis of many examples of this furring is that it costs almost as much as the joists because of all the cutting and fitting of small pieces. The engineered floor trusses (less pieces) can be installed quickly. Engineered I-Joists (Fig. 6.6) can also be installed quickly, but they have limitations for the large HVAC plenum zones. However, they are fine for the smaller plumbing and electrical wiring runs. At printing time, 2× joists cost about $1.00/linear foot, I-joists cost about $1.50/linear foot and engineered floor joists cost about $3.00/lineal foot. One other obvious advantage, if one is making a true apple-to-apple comparison of electrical wiring and plumbing costs, they generally cost less with floor trusses. With our ranch-on-basement design, a large portion of the wiring is in this easier working zone. A smart, higher-volume residential firm will not only see these installation cost benefits, but will be experienced to capitalize on them. (For example, their wiring labor costs should be less costly.) By factor-

ing the installation ease, less waste, less human error and other advantages of the floor trusses, it's easy to see the value of using engineered trusses.

One other value of engineered trusses vs. standard lumber trusses is that you can build larger, more useful rooms (in the ranch design, this means better rooms at both main and basement levels) that are chopped up less because longer spans are possible with engineered trusses. One interesting point is that the code minimum for floors allows for L/180 flexing. This means that a 15' floor (180") can bow downward up to 1" and still be safe. The engineered I-joist product is also a good product here and enables longer spans. However, my experience, some builders sensing, as well as some owner's experiences, is that this code-safe seems "bouncy". This seems to indicate cheapness, even though within safe limits. I agree. Some homes also are built with wider, 19.2" on-center spacing (which uses less material) rather than the typical 16" on-center spacing. The tops of the engineered trusses are 3½" wide and the "cost effective" 2× joists are only 1½" wide. This means that the span gap between solid material at the top nail-

Figure 6.16 Floor trusses.

ing point is less (12½" vs. 14½"). Which floor feels more secure and which one has a better hit ratio of nailing and gluing even using the same high-quality sub-flooring, like ¾"-thick AdvanTech? I am more conservative in the span values than the engineered truss software allows for this "feel" issue.

I use this flooring structural improvement by integrating it with another of my design guidelines. Most of your *preferred* basement space will be toward the daylight zones (windows) and the utility functions (stairs, utility rooms, bathrooms and closets) should be against the bermed concrete foundation walls. Since these usage areas in the basement and above on the main floor are similar, you will need dividing walls. We plan for the basement framing in the designing of the project. We split this 26' span into a, say, 15' section (span) and an 11' foot section. The 15' section is towards the view side (daylight zone) and is probably a bedroom. Since we have installed the vertical dividing wall in the basement near the middle of the 26' span, we can use 18"-high engineered trusses. Looking at this another way, if we try to "save" the mid-wall cost and use stronger, 24"-high floor trusses for the

full 26', the floor will not feel as solid. Anyway, you will likely add a dividing wall in the basement later.

A lesser span may provide the elimination of this mid-wall. In the great room of the EnergyStar Model home (see Figure 12.1), note the home's 20' width. Typically the mid-wall is not needed here, which means a potential den in the basement of up to 20' wide and 36' long (see Figure 6.16).

The type of flooring used on the main floor affects how the trusses should be set. If ceramic tile is used in the kitchen area, a stiffer floor is needed to minimize flexing (or bounce) or the tile joints will crack. I have friends who have "saved" on the reduced floor structure and had to pay to have the tile repaired.

One other floor structural issue is the choice of installing radiant-heating flooring, especially using concrete flooring. Let's assume that this radiant-heating, concrete floor is on the view side of the 15' section of the house. This structure will likely need to be steel-based, with different technical issues. Nevertheless, the utilities in the back 11' area can use engineered floor trusses to carry the HVAC plenums. These plenums will fan out and downward in size to feed the concrete/steel areas and can still fit into the smaller overhead zone of the now-required, heavier steel I-beams which may be only 8" high.

HEATING AND COOLING

Now that we have developed a good building envelope, we can address the mechanical heating and cooling aspects (HVAC) of the home. Since many of these last-home structures will be in temperate climates (these are the growth regions), and we have a modest-sized home, I prefer a high-efficiency heat pump. In colder climates, local energy sources such as gas-based fuels may be needed, but let's start with the heat pump. With American high-tech ingenuity refining electronic controls and a valid push for less atmosphere harming refrigerants (LEED points), heat-pump development will continue to evolve positively. Geo-thermal heat pumps are also available. Seek the advice of a respected HVAC sub-contractor to help you make the proper choices for your home.

Another variation of a heat pump is a dual-source heat pump. If you already have gas fuel for your hot water heating, the heat pump "backup" could be gas when the temperature drops to around 30-35°. Then, instead of the less-efficient, emergency, electric heat strips boosting the heat output, the back-up gas source comes on. This back-up system, like the more expensive electric heat strips, is on for brief periods of large energy demands. An averaging affect is in play. Heat pumps have become more efficient (they work better now to draw heat when it's colder outside) and their cross-over payback is now so good that the need for the emergency heat strips is minimized. In some lower-to-middle-American temperature zones, in a modest-sized home, the emergency heat strips may not be needed.

Typically, most HVAC sub-contractors over-size the HVAC system needed in a home. Local and national technical guides are available for specifics, but realize that the sizing needs to be closer to the reality of this better-built home. The HVAC system needs to on-and-off cycle at a consistent rate. Not on most of the time or off most of the time. Variable speed air-handlers are a good choice. Cycling time is also needed for proper humidity control. Remember that those expensive windows and more-costly insulation help pay for this smaller, better heat

pump (or pumps). This strategy is not frequently employed in American residential construction.

An example of this HVAC over-sizing syndrome appears to be developing on the guest-house project at press time. The comparison of this 519 sq. ft. guest house to the 1550 sq. ft. Walnut Mountain EnergyStar house noted earlier is relevant here. First, both houses have almost identical Timber Truss, super-foam panel roofs, R19 spray-foam exterior walls, basement layout, etc. The only minor differences is that the little guest house uses a modest $5/12 \times 21.5'$ truss and the guest house has more framed 2×6 (R19), non-bermed basement walls. The lower pitched truss nets an inside cathedral peak of around 13' vs. the Walnut House which is about 15' high. The guest house has less air volume due to the more modest ceiling. They are about 15 air miles apart in similar mountain terrain and positioning. They both have and will use high-grade, EnergyStar rated, dual pane, low-E windows. The largest group of windows on the guest house is on the East side, but it will have hardwood trees to add shading. The two small West gable windows (casement style, 2'×3' each which totals 12 sq. ft.) are well under the roof porch roof and will also have some summer hardwood tree shading. Thus, no unwanted summer solar heat gain occurs on this side. The ratio of windows to floor space is close. The Walnut House has a higher ratio of windows on the winter heat-loaded North side. Note the almost perfect 3-to-1 ratio between these two projects. The Walnut House energy numbers and sizing are presented later in detail. But for quick reference here, the Walnut House has a mid-level efficiency Trane heat pump rated at 3 tons (about 36,000 BTU's) for both the main floor and the mostly finished basement (totals almost 2,800 sq. ft. of conditioned space). My gut feel for this guest house before verifying with RESCHECK software as a check or manually calculating the heat load, is that the load should be about 12-14,000 BTU's. This is a little more than a ton unit or even a $1^1/_4$ ton unit. However, not many sizes are offered below $1^1/_2$ tons in many of the heat pump product lines. A super-efficient 1 ton unit may even work just fine.

When the general contractor received the initial quotation back from his HVAC sub-contractor, the size was far different than my estimate. We assume that both the general contractor and his HVAC sub-contractor are experienced professionals. But how can a house one-third the size using nearly-identical, high-quality construction (EnergyStar) techniques be so far apart? The HVAC guy estimated we needed a 2-ton unit for this guest house. Let's see — one-third size means two-thirds the heating/cooling load — I don't get it. I'm concerned that we will not only pay 33% to 50% more for an HVAC unit than we need and that the system will be *short cycling*. That is, the heat pump will not run long enough per cycle to reach the optimum performance level (several minutes or more). Also, it likely will not fully de-humidify the air as the condensation in the air handler may not be evacuated fully. So, we shall monitor this project to see it through to a good resolution for the client.

FRESH AIR INPUT

A related topic to the HVAC system and our now "tight house" is the need for a fresh air input. LEED refers to this as *mechanical ventilation*. This is the way we make the house actually breathe. We need fresh air coming into the house to constantly flush the air environment for healthy living. There are two approaches to achieve this air quality and they are linked to the size of the home: First, on modest-sized homes, like the EnergyStar House in Chapter 12, a motorized damper controlling a small, 4"- to 6"-diameter vent to a preferred external wall location is needed. This damper is activated when the HVAC air handler blower is running. Fresh air is brought into the air handler directly. Figure 6.17 shows this damper concept and how it relates to the general HVAC system.

Let's make a comparison of this *introduced* 4" leak compared to an average home and an to an even older breathing home like we used to build (and probably most of you live in). Estimates used to show the size of typical air leaks will help the reader visualize the effective diameter of all the infiltration points (air leaks) in houses of different levels of construction quality. Let's estimate the leak-equivalent-diameter of a well-built, tight, home may

be close to the size of a basketball. An average constructed house's diameter is closer to a large trash can. And even worse, an older, poorly sealed home may have the diameter equivalent of 4' to 6'! Thus, our poor little 4"-diameter fresh-air-intake "leak" seems to pale compared to these monster holes. Figure 6.18 shows one of those leaky little devils.

When you consider the effect of air pressure on the entire home, things are worse without this fresh air intake. Here's analogy used by a SouthFace instructor at a recent Georgia Energy Code seminar that helped his audience get the point. He assumed that the HVAC system has about a 1,000cfm (cubic feet per minute) air flow rate. Our little fresh-air leak, controlled damper, is allowing 50cfm to be injected into the house. Since the HVAC air handler creates a negative pressure (outside air wants to come into the house) when running, existing air leaks throughout the structure would naturally allow air (pressure) to come into the home. This air could come from any source near the leak. A leaky garage wall (carbon monoxide, oils, gas scent, etc.) or a hot attic (or cold in the winter) or a plumbing stack may vent fumes. This 50cfm has to come from somewhere. With the fresh air controlled, the effective negative pressure of the house is reduced to the extent that any remaining unknown leaks in the home are minimized.

I don't know of any residential designers, architects or builders who can specify exactly where the leaks in the house are located. I can't. I'm not smart enough to do this. However, I can design a tight, well-sealed structure with the smallest leaks that can be built and then install this controlled leak (a fresh air damper pipe) where I want it.

The average size home in America is about 2,000 sq. ft. and a more expensive solution for fresh air intake is likely needed. The fresh air damper will have a small energy loss penalty (a few dollars a month in energy costs). This controlled leak is a relatively small price to pay to give us fresh air. However, as the house size increases, to gain fresh air, this energy loss penalty increases. The crossover

> We need fresh air coming into the house to constantly flush the air's environment for healthy living.

point is in the range of 1600 sq. ft. and will require ERVs and HRVs. For simplicity, we will use the Southern-climate-specified ERV (Energy Recovery Ventilator) vs. the Northern-climate-version HRV (Heat Recovery Ventilator). They are similar, but the ERV system is optimized for cooling and de-humidifying. The HRV is designed for supplying heat-load needs. Figure 6.19 shows how the physical unit appears as a stand-alone device. Both ventilator types will exchange the energy you already have in the house air with the new fresh air coming into the house and not lose the energy already generated. Figure 6.21 shows the ERV installed within a typical HVAC system.

The increased cost for the larger house is about $1500-$2000 installed. Thus, for about 1 percent or less of the entire house's budget, your family will be breathing fresh air. The beautiful granite countertops, nor the picturesque designer claw-foot bathtub in front of the huge picture window in your dream bathroom can't do this for your family. We all have our priorities, so it's your decision.

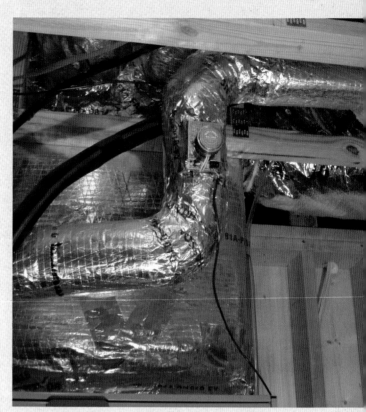

Figure 6.18 Fresh air intake damper.

Figure 6.17 Fresh air intake vent.

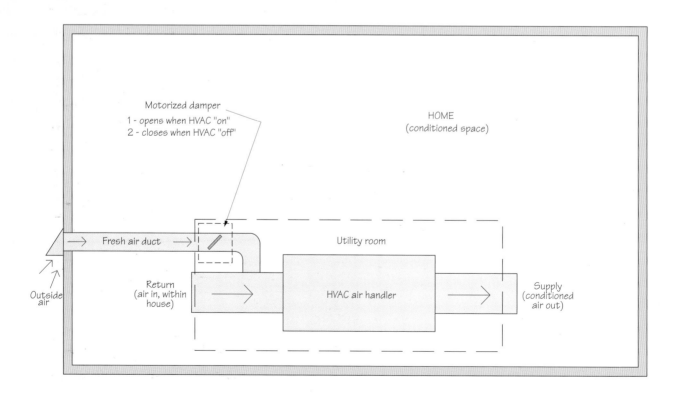

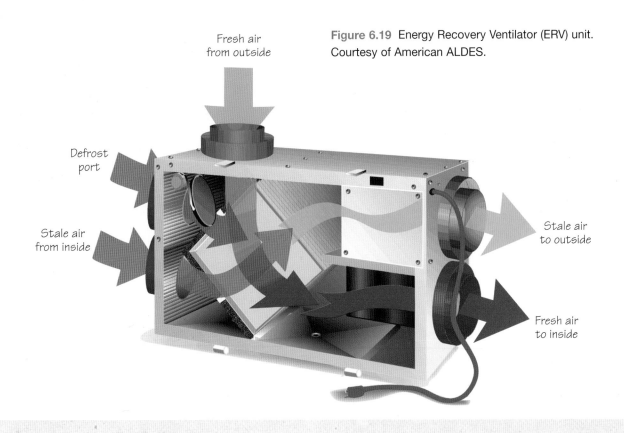

Fresh air
from outside

Defrost
port

Stale air
from inside

Stale air
to outside

Fresh air
to inside

Figure 6.19 Energy Recovery Ventilator (ERV) unit. Courtesy of American ALDES.

FIREPLACES AND STOVES

Back-up heat sources such as fireplaces and stoves will be important for our energy future. In colder areas, wood-burning stoves and maybe pellet fueled units are candidates. You should do some research on fireplaces. Because of the cosmetic lure of fireplaces, tight, good sealing doors are hard to find. A tight sealing door to the combustion zone and a direct air intake for the burning are minimums. The stove also needs this air intake, despite what some of the stove technologies say. If you have difficulty finding a good solution, search for units meeting the tougher R2000 Canadian standards.

I don't like vent-free stoves because they take air out of your living space to fuel the combustion. If you have built a tight, well-insulated home, where will this air come from for the combustion? One of my local chimney-sweep friends says that these *free* stoves are restricted in some states. Didn't our parents tell us, more than once, about free stuff? Look for *direct vent* stoves and fireplaces. They have the combustion chamber sealed to the living space and the air to feed the burning comes down piping while expelling the combustion wastes in another isolated layer of the pipe. They cost more, but remember, now you don't need a big unit.

Figure 6.20 Direct-combustion air intake for fireplace.

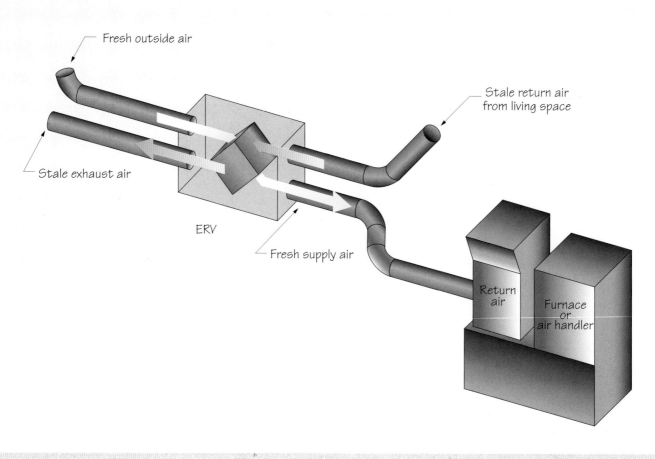

Fresh outside air

Stale exhaust air

ERV

Fresh supply air

Stale return air
from living space

Return
air

Furnace
or
air handler

Figure 6.21   ERV within an HVAC system. Courtesy of ConsERV.

Figure 6.22   Cutaway of Opal 2 fireplace.

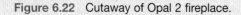

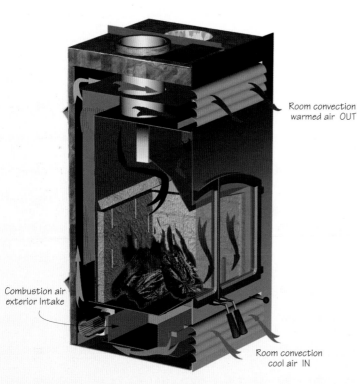

Room convection
warmed air OUT

Combustion air
exterior Intake

Room convection
cool air IN

HOT WATER HEATING

Heating water, particularly with electric-source power, can be a nice chunk of your monthly bill — about 25-35 percent. So, it is important to improve the efficiency of the hot-water heater if you will be using electricity to heat the water. I prefer the long-life, aptly named, Marathon hot-water heater from RUUD. Not only does this unit have super foam insulated walls, it has a life-time tank. Figure 6.23 shows the outside shape of the Marathon, which is different than the typical flat-top unit. The cut-away drawing notes the key functional details that lead to its higher performance. The average life of a typical tank water heater in the U.S. is about eight years. The Marathon lasts at least *twice* that long, but only costs twice as much as the typical water heater.

Temperature and
pressure relief valve

All-plastic tank

Fill tube

Thermally fused upper
heating element

Tough molded polyethylene
outer jacket

2¹/₂" Envirofoam®
insulation

Long-lasting stainless steel
incoloy lower element

Recessed brass drain valve

Figure 6.23 Marathon water heater from RUUD and cutaway details.

Small electric tankless water heaters may be a good option to consider for different areas of your home and they have almost a lifetime existence. The large electrical central units, used to supply the entire house, have large power demands, possibly using three, 50-amp circuit breakers.

ENERGY-EFFICIENCY FORMAL PROGRAMS

There are two good formal programs that provide a way to measure and validate energy-efficiency strategies: EnergyStar and the USGBC's LEED-For-Homes program. EnergyStar is summarized page 76, as is the LEED/Homes on page 77.

Building codes are the *minimum* that is required and isn't a *quality control process* as in other industries. If you dig, you'll find that most building code officials will tell you that they are not checking for "quality". What? Most manufactured products in the United States and around the world have formal quality control systems. If your professional life is only in the residential construction industry, you may not be aware of this. The vehicle you drove to work today and the electronic, 64-bit audio CD system make your life better than you realize because of *quality control*. These industries design, test and monitor their products far above what we do for our most expensive purchase — our homes. Besides the keyword *formal* another keyword is *testing*. The formal issue is to establish a set of standards and the testing is validation that the product meets those standards.

Let us stress that the testing needs to be third-party, not your brother-in-law who needs a job. For example, a well-accepted premise now in any

ENERGYSTAR * ABBREVIATED SUMMARY

1. EFFECTIVE INSULATION: (North Georgia example – see local code)

HOUSE ZONE	" R" VALUE NEEDED	COMMENTS
CEILING/ROOF	R30 (or 38)	Typ. SIP roofs = R31, or R40
FRAMED WALLS	R19 (or 13)	Typ. SIP walls = R24
FLOOR	R9	Not needed with "Ranch on Basement"
BASEMENT WALL	R11	Framed wall section = R19 (better)
FOUNDATION WALL	R5	Prefer R10 external to concrete

2. HIGH PERFORMANCE WINDOWS: (North Georgia example – see local code)

ITEM	VALUE NEEDED	COMMENTS
NO. OF GLASS PANES	Double Pane	Also Low-E needed, Argon filled ?
INSULATING VALUE	U.40	= R2.5 (minimum)
SOLAR HEAT GAIN (SHGC)	.40	Lower is better with hotter climate

3. TIGHT CONSTRUCTION & DUCTS:

ITEM	REQUIRED	COMMENTS
A - DUCTS IN CONDITIONED SPACES	(within building envelope)	Not in crawl spaces or hot attics
B - SEALED DUCTS	Metal tape (UL181) or mastic	Not use "duct" tape !
C - INSULATED DUCTS	R6- R8	Must be insulated also (like house)
D - RIGHT SIZE DUCTS	Per ACCA MANUAL "D" & "J"	See qualified HVAC contractor

4. EFFICIENT HEATING & COOLING EQUIPMENT:

ITEM	REQUIRED	COMMENTS
A – PROPER SYSTEM SIZING	Per ACCA MANUAL "S" & "J"	Not too big, not too small
B – PROPER EQUIPMENT PLACEMENT	(within building envelope)	Not in crawl spaces or hot attics
C – PROPER REFRIGERANT CHARGE	Check at end of installation	Low charge drops efficiency
D – CORRECT AIRFLOW	Check for leaks and flow rate	For better system operation
E – MECHANICAL VENTILATION	Fresh air input 4" duct/damper	Larger House = ERV or HRV

5. EFFICIENT PRODUCTS:

ITEM	REQUIRED	COMMENTS
A – QUALIFIED APPLIANCES	Refrigerators, Dishwashers, Clothes Washers & Dryers	See www.energystar.gov for list
B – QUALIFIED LIGHTING	Compact Fluorescent bulbs (CFL's) as possible	See www.energystar.gov for list
C – ADVANCED LIGHTING PACKAGE	50-100% of fixtures bulbs, & fans are on approved list	See www.energystar.gov for list
D – HIGH EFFICENCY WATER HEATING	Storage (tank), tank-less, heat pump, or Solar types	See www.energystar.gov for list

6. THIRD PARTY VERIFICATION:

ITEM	REQUIRED	COMMENTS
NORMAL HOME ENERGY RATING	HER rating per plans	Software simulation of insulation values
OR: BUILDER OPTION PACKAGE	Build per Set Guidelines	Guidelines per climate region
FIELD VERIFICATION AT HOME	Reviews actual & tests	Actually checks insulation, ducts, etc.
BLOWER DOOR TEST	ACH less than .35	Air exchange per Hour (leakage)

* Summarized from EPA (U.S. ENVIRONMENTAL PROTECTION AGENCY) web page

See www.energystar.gov web page for details

LEED FOR HOMES * ABBREVIATED SUMMARY

NO. BEDROOMS : _____ FLOOR AREA (SF): _____

ITEM NO.	TITLE	DESCRIPTION	MAX. POINTS
Innovation and Design Process (ID)--------------------------------------			9
ID1.1---1.3	Integrated Project Planning	Integrated Project Team, Charette	2
ID2.1---2.4	Quality Management for Durability	Durability plan, Quality, 3rd Party Inspct.	3
ID3.1---3.4	Innovative/Regional Design	Description/Justification of Measures	4
		Points Awarded →	
Location and Linkages (LL) --			10
LL2	Site Selection	Avoid Sensitive Sites & Farmland	2
LL3.1---3.3	Preferred Locations	Edge, Infill, or Previous Develop. Site	2
LL4	Infrastructure	Within ½ mile existing Water & Sewer	1
LL5.1---5.3	Community Resource & Public Transit	Community Resources/Public Transit	3
LL6	Access to Open Space	Publicly Accessible Green Spaces	1
		Points Awarded →	
Sustainable Sites (SS) --			21
SS1.1---1.2	Site Stewardship	Erosion Control, Min. Site Disturbance	1
SS2.1---2.4	Landscaping	No Evasive plants, Limit turf, drought	7
SS3	Shading of Hardscapes	Trees for Hardscape Shading	1
SS4.1---4.2	Surface Water Management	Permeable, Permanent Erosion Control	6
SS5	Non-Toxic Pest Control	Pest Control Alternatives from list	2
SS6.1---6.3	Compact Development	Avg. House Density 10,20/Acre	4
		Points Awarded →	
Water Efficiency (WE) ---			15
WE1.1---1.2	Water Re-Use	Rainwater Harvesting, Greywater Reuse	5
WE2.1---2.3	Irrigation System	High Eff., 3rd Party verify, Professional	4
WE3.1---3.2	Indoor Water Use	High or Very High Efficiency Fixtures	6
		Points Awarded →	
Energy & Atmosphere (EA) ---			38
EA2.1-2.2	EnergyStar Home	Exceeds EnergyStar, 3rd party testing	34
EA7.1-7.2	Water Heating	Improved water heating, Pipe insulation	3
EA11	Refrigeration Management	Minimize Ozone Depletion, Warming	1
		Points Awarded →	
Materials & Resources (MR) ---			14
MR1.1---1.3	Material Efficient Framing	Advanced Framing or SIP's	3
MR2.1---2.2	Environmental Preferable Products	Tropical woods (FSC),Material from List	8
MR3.1---3.2	Waste Management	Document, Reduce Waste 25-100%,	3
		Points Awarded →	
Indoor Air Quality IEQ) ---			20
IEQ1	EnergyStar with IAP	Indoor Air Package w/ EnergyStar	11
IEQ2.1---2.2	Combustion Venting	Space Heating, High Peform, Fireplace	2
IEQ3	Moisture Control	Analyze Moisture Loads, System ?	1
IEQ4.1---4.3	Outdoor Air Ventilation	ASHRAE 62.2, Heat Recovery, Testing	3
IEQ5.1---5.3	Local Exhaust	ASHRAE 62.2, Bathroom Exh., Testing	2
IEQ6.1---6.2	Supply Air Distribution	ACCA Manual D, 3rd Party Testing Flow	2
IEQ7.1---7.3	Supply Air Filtering	8,10,13 MERV Filters, Adequate Flow	2
IEQ8.1---8.2	Contaminant Control	Seal Ducts, Walk Mats, Flush 1 week	4
IEQ9.1---9.2	Radon Protection	Install Radon vent, EPA Zone 1 or Not	1
IEQ10.1---10.4	Garage Pollutant Protection	No ducts, tight seal, Detached Garage	3
		Points Awarded →	
Awareness & Education (AE) ---			3
AE1.1---1.3	Education – Homeowner/Tenants	Manual, Walkthrough, LEED Awareness	2
AE2.1	Education – Building Managers	Building Mgr. manual, Walkthrough	1
		Points Awarded →	

CERTIFIED = 45	SILVER = 60	GOLD = 75	PLATINUM = 90	MAXIMUM POINTS = 130

TOTAL POINTS AWARDED FOR HOME → _____

* Courtesy of USGBC (US Green Building Council), See usgbc.org web page for details

manufacturing environment is that the production group that is building the product *is not the one who inspects* the product. It must be an independent group, now typically called the QC (quality control) department. Check typical manufacturing corporations internal organizational charts and you will find that the QC guys do not report to the manufacturing/production guys. They are independent and their leadership meets at the top. We don't do this process in residential construction. We do not want the "fox guarding the hen house". The EnergyStar program for Energy issues is conducted by the United States EPA division and the LEED-FOR-HOMES by the US Building Green Council (USGBC) for quality home construction, in my opinion, both are solid programs to embrace this proven approach to deliver a quality product. There are also some regional and city/county programs that are excellent, such as the Atlanta-based

Southface's Earthcraft program (done in conjunction with the Atlanta area NAHB group). But for a more universal scope, I'll focus on EnergyStar and LEED/HOMES.

If you survey the elements in the brief summary of the EnergyStar program on page 76, some familiar terms will emerged based upon my earlier points. Note also that my comments section gives clues, practical applications or key trigger elements as to the item's importance. The big picture of this formal page of "stuff to do" is that you cannot have a quality home, from an energy perspective, without doing most of these things. Conversely, if you do achieve most of theses steps in your home, you very likely cannot produce a "bad home". I say that this means quality. For more details for the serious folks, please go to the EPA Web page and delve into what makes energy quality happen.

Now as we move to the LEED-FOR-HOMES summary on page 77, now-familiar terms are also evident. In section EA (Energy and Atmosphere), the EnergyStar program appears. Note that the 34 EnergyStar program points are most of the 45 points to qualify a home under LEED. The linking of these two programs is a validation of the LEED's approach. Note when third party testing is required (remember, not your brother-in-law) and that there are several categories, like EA, that address subsystems within the home. Points are awarded for each category achieved. This process has evolved from the successful USGBC's LEED program now used in many commercial and city/government building programs. An important concept is usually missed in both programs, particularly for the residential market, and is triggered by the "that costs too much" response. Think how much an air bag system costs for a car. If you want to save money, take it out. (You can for *your* car, but not mine.) The automotive industry is *formal* and *tests* their products. Without the air bag in your car, the actual test occurs when you, well, you know.

Figure 6.26 Blower door test in process. Photo courtesy of Infiltec Corp.

BLOWER DOOR TEST

One last testing idea that is critical to the third-party concept and ensures that quality exists in the home that your are mortgaging your future on — blower door test. Look at the EnerygyStar chart page 76 and note the bottom-line entry for blower door test. A certified technician attaches a

Figure 6.27
Home system
with door testing.
Illustration cour-
tesy of Retrotec.

mechanism to one of the house's exterior doors and pressurizes the house. Figure 6.26 shows what the setup looks like during the test.

The door assembly, with the air gauges in the mechanism, can indicate the pressure drop within the house due to air leaks. The certified techni-cian compares the house's dimensions with the gauge data and calculates an ACH (Air exChange per Hour) figure. This figure means, relative to the volume of the house, how much air leaking every hour from or into the home. The EnergyStar value, as noted in the summary, has a figure of .35. This means that if you can get your leaks down to about one-third of the house's volume per hour, it is a "good house". For fun, think back to our fresh air damper discussion and the relative sizes of leaks for different levels of quality. The blower door test formalizes this technical fact and is both measurable and validating. Figure 6.27 shows the house as a *system* while doing the blower door test.

As you look at specific items within the LEED summary, you can see that there is an abbreviation system within the categories for specific points. This may seem too formal or complicated or what-ever. However, the beauty here is that manufactur-ers can now focus their efforts to make products

to address these needs within their specific exper-tise. This works well in the proven commercial LEED programs. Isn't capitalism wonderful? The sub-program for Energystar points can move you toward the overall goal of LEED certification. You, the client, gets to chose, within reason, where your effort and dollar emphasis is placed to reach your desired level of certification (Certified, Silver, Gold, Platinum). If your system to measure the quality is so low that a home not meeting at least EnergyStar level in the energy category, you will not have quality. But beyond this base level of expected quality, each client or homebuilder can choose their areas of enhancement. In some regions, water saving, the WE category becomes more sig-nificant. For example, using active solar panels on the roof for heating water will award more points in EA7.1 and .2. We all should be sensitive to the SS (Sustainable Sites) category, as most of us have experienced the crazy growth of suburbia and the resulting tree clearing. This SS focus is also an important measure of quality (of life). LEED-FOR-HOMES is a viable, valid and needed program that has potential for Americans to own quality homes — and not drive around without an airbag just to "save money".

07

Casual-Cabin/Timber Style

Now we are going into my bias zone.

With the growing stress in American lifestyle for pursuit of consumerism, the MegaTrend of *Soft-Touch* is  being validated constantly. Not only do stressed families want to get away from the rat race for the weekend, they frequently choose a more casual cabin with a "woodsy" feel in a less urban/suburban area. There is something special walking through the door into a wood or even log cabin. However, a weekend is just a short period of time. Over time, balance is needed for even this soft-touch of a wood interior.

The cabin "feel" concept guides the decision process in a majority of home seekers in our region, in both second homes and specifically planned retirement homes. In fact, some feedback received on one my designs via the realtor was that the house was better suited as a retirement home and not really a "cabin". It had significant wood on the interior, but some clients wanted *everything* to be natural wood.

TIMBER-STYLE TYPES

With this in mind, I moved toward timber-like style structures as the basis for future homes. To help the reader, I'll present three basic homes of timber styles. First the classic *timber frame* concept that is well known to anyone that has looked at building magazines or vacationed in mountain areas. This traditional framing technique stems from our European craftsman roots. Basically, a large cross section of the structure, called a *bent* (using larger wood beams — the less/more concept) is usually hand crafted. Some companies now are also using high-tech NC (Numerical Controlled) equipment to cut these wood beams. The *This Old House* television show introduction is a great example of timber framing. A key and positive element to current timber framing suppliers is that they are typically using SIPs (structural insulated panels) as the wall covering. They utilize them in a curtain wall technique — the well-designed, strong-structured, beautiful wood bent is the structural frame that the SIPs are attached to. Interior pictures of this type framing will show vertical posts visible every 8' to 10'. As a result, only a few beams are needed to frame a house (less/more). The SIP's are utilized for both the walls and roofs. This roof construction is inherently non-vented. These homeowners almost universally attest to the comfort and energy-saving results they provide. The client can finish the ceiling interior with a variety of materials, from thinner tongue-and-groove wood decking to sheetrock. The sheetrock option provides an opportunity to use complementary colors to temper the wood look in some rooms. My experience shows this classic timber-framing style costs about 50% more per square foot than typical stud-wall construction.

Heavy rafter-beam construction frequently shows up in weekend cabins. This lower-grade approach

---

Figure 7.1 Wood beam ceiling (4×6 exposed).

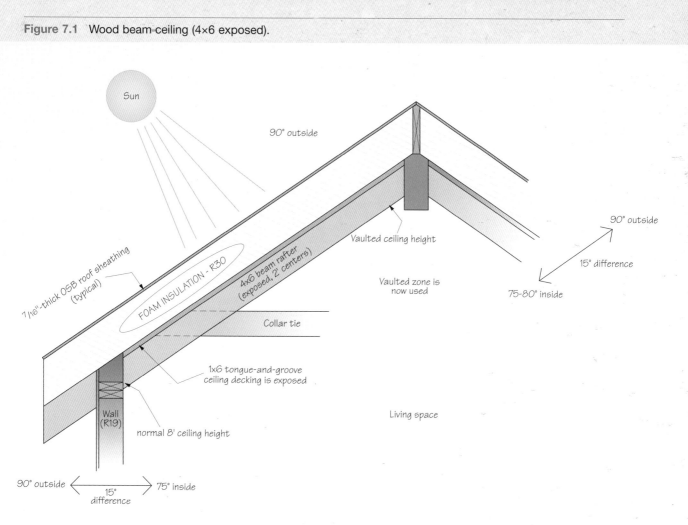

Figure 7.2 Exposed 6×6 ceiling beams.

Figure 7.3 4×8 beams and thicker 2×6 T&G decking.

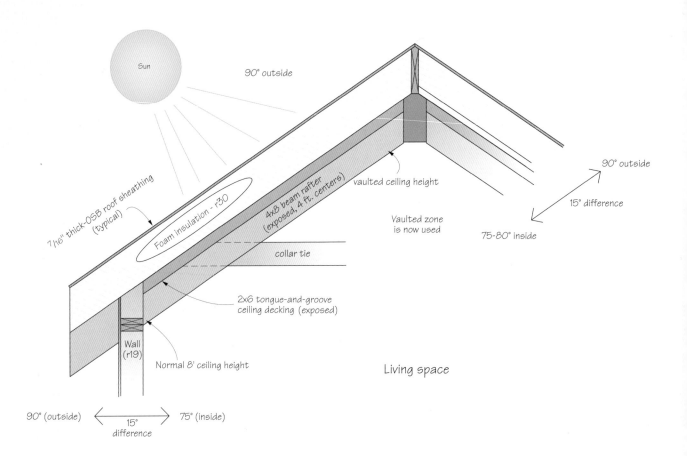

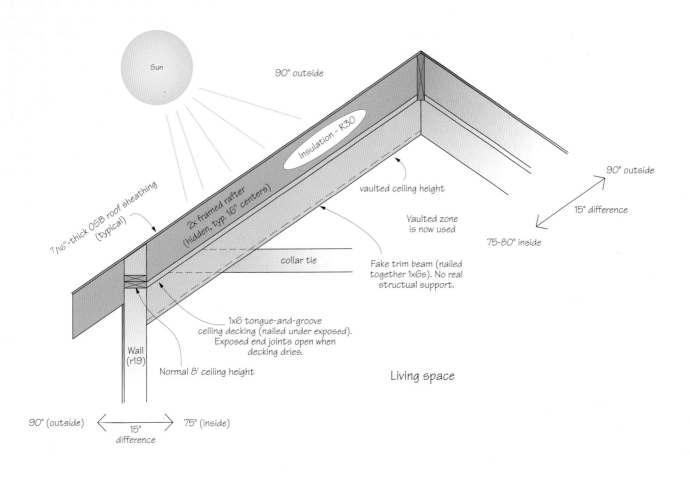

Figure 7.4 Fake beams.

uses 4×6 or 4×8 pine or douglas fir wood, on 2' to 4' spacings as *exposed* rafters as shown in Figure 7.1. (After all, you want to see them.) Figure 7.2 shows larger 6×6 pine beams on 2' centers with 1×6 wood decking (in this case cypress) nailed on top of the structural beams. A quality approach is to use 2×6 tongue-and-groove decking on top these beams and make a non-vented, SIP roof. Figure 7.3 shows the technique of using 4×8 beams with a wider spacing of 4' (using less beams) and the thicker roof decking. The bulk of the stick framing, mainly the walls, is framed in studs. This exposed wood beam approach costs about 10 percent more than regular rafters. This technique still requires the manual cutting and nailing, at the site, a number of individual rafters, cross-connecting collar tie beams, etc.

This exposed wood beam rafter approach has some cosmetic vs. structure decision ramifications. In Figure 7.1 and Figure 7.3, note that the collar tie beams are recommended. These horizontal beams are frequently needed in these open-style rooms.

A normal two-story house with a full second floor has these structural elements already in the second floor joists. That is, they complete the triangle of tying the two opposing walls together with the roof rafters — the other two sides of the triangle. A triangle is a strong structural element. If you do not use these collar ties in an open vaulted zone, the ridge supporting beam has to be engineered larger to compensate for the allowable L/240 sag (for example, on a 20' [240"] open great room, the ridge beam is allowed to sag 1"). Here is where cosmetic and structure can collide. If the client's great room is a steep pitched roof, say 12/12 pitch, this means that if this ridge sag occurs, without the collar beams (or wind beams) the wall has to move out 1" horizontally. Since it is a 1 to 1 (12/12) relationship, and we know energy and matter are not destroyed, something has to give. The roof and the walls will move. The cosmetic half of this is that some people don't like the look of these beams "in the way". If the beams are higher up, closer to the ridge than

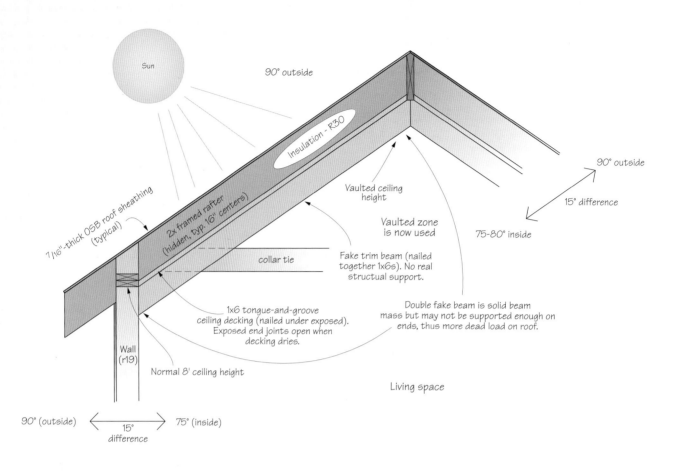

Sun

90° outside

Insulation - R30

7/16"-thick OSB roof sheathing (typical)

2x framed rafter (hidden, typ. 16" centers)

Vaulted ceiling height

Vaulted zone is now used

collar tie

Fake trim beam (nailed together 1x6s). No real structual support.

90° outside

15° difference

75-80° inside

1x6 tongue-and-groove ceiling decking (nailed under exposed). Exposed end joints open when decking dries.

Double fake beam is solid beam mass but may not be supported enough on ends, thus more dead load on roof.

Wall (r19)

Normal 8' ceiling height

Living space

90° (outside)   75° (inside)
        15°
    difference

Figure 7.5   Double-fake beams.

the eave (side wall top plate), they won't be effective. Any structural engineer or building inspector will tell you that the beams must be below one-third of the distance from the eave to the ridge, which means they are lower in the roof vertical dimension. Some people feel closed in by these larger beams at the preferred structural height. The raised collar beam version, only 12" to 24" above the top wall plate is a good compromise. In all well engineered truss-type structures, either conventional 2×4 trusses or the larger timber framing version, the collar issue is usually incorporated properly. I have noticed this not happening when the cosmetic feel overpowers the conserva-

The classic *timber frame* concept is well known to anyone that has looked at building magazines or vacationed in mountain areas.

tive design rules. For example, in a 32'-wide great room with a 12/12 (or steeper) roof pitch that has a small timber truss in the top third near the ridge. The bottom of the truss is about 10' above the wall plate, say 18' or 19' off the floor. This beautiful hand-crafted wood beam truss, physically smaller, is way up near the top so that its beauty is lost. Does cosmetic win or lose? Hey, what was that creaking noise in the roof?

In the fake-beam style, the upper roof structure is conventionally framed with cutting rafters on 16" centers or pre-engineered wood trusses on 2' centers. (See Figure 7.4.) Typically, the interior finished is nailed from the underside, which can be wood or sheetrock.

The fake part are the box beams, which are made from smaller 1× wood and are cosmetic trim, not structural. The concept of less/more shows up here and is usually not considered in cost comparisons. If you used the timber-truss approach, the thicker 2×6 tongue-and-groove decking (about $2.00 per sq. ft.) should be nailed on top of the structural beam. The thinner 1×6 or 1×8 decking (about $1.00 per sq. ft.) is typically nailed underneath. This underneath labor requires more cuts and working upside down. The increased labor costs of the thinner wood is a good down payment toward the thicker wood decking *top* material cost. All those joints that meticulously are put together with a quality trim carpenter's knowledge (and more labor) of using overlapped 45° cuts will lose to Mother Nature.

With normal HVAC performance, and even with high-quality, low-moisture (10 percent) decking, these joints will open up. And, since they are longitude-based, gaps are inevitable. This entire cosmetic-driven decision has some not-so-nice wood "effects" that you can enjoy forever.

One more aspect of this "alleged" cost savings of thinner wood material is seen in the process of building a covered porch. A fair assumption is that the porch detail and cosmetic appearance is not as visible or demanding as in the great room or master bedroom. OK with this? We typically use 2×6s decking for a true beam approach and reality demonstrates that not all the wood in your 2×6 bundle is the best. We take some time, not usually done by the typical builder and set aside the less

Figure 7.6 Lack of wood-on-wood contrast.

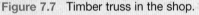

Figure 7.7 Timber truss in the shop.

Figure 7.8 Timber truss with decking on top.

cosmetic 2×6 decking. We use the best pieces in the more obvious rooms, like the *great room* and the poorer pieces in closets, etc. We have ordered enough material, with spares to cover one of the porch roofs with 2×6s. Someone is shouting "Why do you use this expensive 2×6 material here?" Since clients choosing this timber look will likely desire their porch roof to have a similar appearance, this pattern follows. What doesn't follow is that if you used the "cheaper" 1×6 version, you have the potential for the roofing nails coming through this thinner decking. The first brilliant suggestion is to put another layer of, cheaper OSB up there. It is not cheaper to add another layer. One more clue, the guy who usually suggests this cost savings? He won't spend the time setting aside the worse decking and your closet ceiling comes out prettier than your great room. Also, ever notice how this same worker's footprints are on the inside of this decking in your great room?

What do you think the real-world chances of a huge house (or any large surface) demonstrating true craftsman over a more modest sized room?

My last fake example really concerns me. In this case, the builder uses large real-wood timbers. But they are attached to the *underside* of a conventional framed and insulated roof structure with typical hand-framing techniques, 16d nails, etc. It had better be lots of nails! Figure 7.5 shows one version of this "double fake". In this case, the goal for cosmetic effect is burdened by these beams not resting on a solid structural base (like the top plate of a wall) and thus adding dead weight pulling down on the roof structure. And not just a little weight.

The warmth of too much wood will fade and become negative in a few years. Having too much of this beige color will dull your view of the inside environment. The beautiful pine GluLam Southern yellow pine) dining table on the pine wood floor in Figure 7.6 blends in with the surrounding wood. The lack of color contrast of the two beautiful objects is too much of a good thing. This situation is compounded by the ceiling timber structure with the matching fir 2×6 roof decking and wood on most of the walls. Having other walls with sheetrock surfaces enables other colors to be used. See Figure 12.9 for an example of how contrasting/complementary colors can work together.

My favorite timber-like technique is one type of a *hybrid* approach I call *timber-truss* style. Our company has focused our efforts in this style, based upon years of looking at and testing the others. Having experience in developing and running a manufacturing division building high-tech products, I knew this experience would be of value in residential construction. First, we have too much hand-fabrication in the field with an acknowledged growing decrease in the craftsman's skills. Second, this hand-framing on site takes too long and the client's most expensive purchase frequently sits out, unprotected in the rain. The magnitude of mildew lawsuits caused by just this building delay in the field is significant. The issue of waste generated at the site (tons per home)

Figure 7.9 Formal trim & timber style.

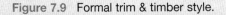

and the landfill issues are well known. We desired a product to fill some of these gaps and still present the customer with a timber-like environment with the warm-wood look being a key component.

Figure 7.7 shows one of our earlier 8/12 × 20' Timber Truss prototypes standing in a display area of our shop. Its location for this shot is significant. It is in a *shop*, completely assembled inside, not shedding water at the building site or falling apart. This particular truss set can be assembled beforehand and safely transported on a matching trailer/building frame to the building site. Our larger 25' and 26' designs are assembled on the site, usually taking one day using a special horizontal table. The table will also jack them up for vertical positioning for the lifting boom truck. Our material concept is to use higher grade GluLam beams, in either the more attractive *architectural* grade or *premium* grade.

Most framing contractors have had experience with the typically available *utility* or *framing* grades. These lower grades are not even close to the appearance of our version. Figure 7.8 shows this truss style installed with the 2×6 ceiling *decking* installed on *top*. Another positive appearance aspect is that GluLam's rarely have checking, bending and twisting that is exhibited in natural wood beams. They can be purchased straight for longer lengths (without loading camber). Even the 6×6 size natural wood beam in Figure 7.2 display normal wood aging characteristics. Guess how much extra labor you "save" by working with these natural wood beams with bow & twist?

The resulting GluLam beam's refined finish allows use in traditional-looking homes (even with crown moulding) as seen in Figure 7.9. The final appearance doesn't have to be "too rustic".

Since GluLams are typically made from Southern yellow pine, a strong and very fast growing tree species, they are considered a good renewable product. With the resulting strength of a GluLam, typically twice that of a typical wood product in most structural engineer's measure values (bend, shear, etc.), smaller beam sizes can be used. With the regional availability of pine trees, the transportation costs of the raw product is reduced. Thus, our base material truly follows *green* concepts. Since we use hard tooling to define the shop detail work, limiting the standard sizes of trusses, and use redundant laser-cut, powder-coated finishes on our steel plates, we achieve some level of productivity of labor for our end product, even in lower volumes. Our truss kits for typical floor plans use as few as seven Timber Trusses and no more than ten (less/more) for the roof structure. Typical Timber Truss kit costs, at press time, were in the $6 to $10 per sq. ft. range. Our goal is to achieve a product that has some level of "modularity" to assist the residential building industry's need to improve and yet be at a reasonable cost.

These Timber trusses sit on either conventional 2×6 framing or SIP walls. With 2×6 framing, we increase the studs at the loading point (typically three). This incremental step adds 32 more studs maximum (about $120 in material) for a typical floor plan. For SIP-based designs, we use a 3×5 GluLam (3⅛" by 5½") at the junction of SIP panels under the truss location. We also double-plate the SIPs on top for more strength. This is one example of how a few steps of a new process will improve residential building quality. We will not improve as an industry unless we get rid of this cheap/big cycle. Something different has to happen. This is our approach to adapt to our own unique market.

We continue planning and experimenting with other SIP variations for future client projects. One project, if it evolves, will use SIP's as large as 8' high by 24' wide that will mesh with our Timber-Truss concept. We hope that one project we're planning will evolve into a LEED FOR HOMES model.

> What do you think the real-world chances of a huge house (or any large surface) demonstrating true craftsman over a more modest sized room?

The Promise of SIP Construction

Structural Insulated Panels (SIPs) have long held the promise as an up-and-coming residential construction concept. We are almost there, particularly for our Last Homes concept. However, overcoming both the sub-contractors inertia to change and burdened with some of  the evils of Dream Houses are slowing the transition. Some hybrid concepts optimizing the use of SIPs, with minor variations, improve their value and can accelerate their adaptation.

As referenced earlier, Michael Morley's book, *Building with Structural Insulated Panels* (SIPs) is an invaluable guide. However, a quickie description of a SIP is appropriate. First, think of a SIP as a large, rectangular-shaped version of an Oreo cookie. The space occupied by the cookies tasteful frosting in the middle is actually an insulating foam product like EPS (Expanded PolyStyrene) or other high-tech foam versions. (Does not taste like an Oreo, however.) The two outer sections forming the sandwich, unlike the cookie dough flavor, is a panel product like OSB (Oriented Strand Board) or CDX plywood (exterior grade). The vendor's bonding process makes these panels strong. The insulation is embedded in the sub-assembly, is universally proven as a higher grade and results in a tighter air-infiltration design. The smallest size is 4'×8' up to monsters 8' wide and 24' long.

Figure 8.1 depicts a basic SIP. You can begin to see the possibilities of applying less/more. Even the 4×8 module is a good building block. There are two popular thicknesses of SIPs: 4" (R15 insulation value with EPS) or 6" (R24 insulation value with EPS). An 8" version is used for roof applications (up to R31 if using EPS foam). They are usually assembled with long, thin, high-strength panel screws that are self-drilling. Thus less screws, more strength and faster assembly at the site.

Figure 8.1   Basic SIP (structural insulated panel).

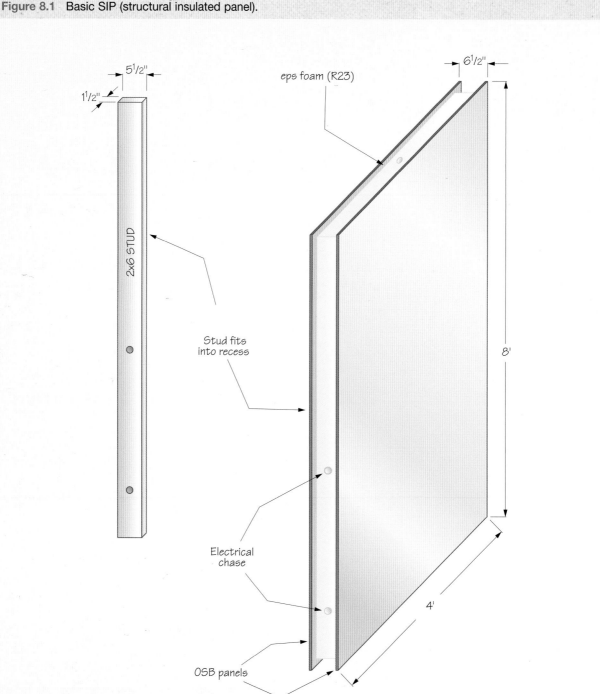

Figure 8.2   SIP walls and timber-truss style.

Morley's book explains the full range of using SIP technology, including larger, more complex homes. My focus is "last homes" (which he also foreshadowed in his work). Our first projects utilizing SIPs, like our Timber-Truss concept, seemed more successful by using a hybrid, not a pure SIP-only approach. Note that classic Timber Frame advertising now alludes to some "hybrid" version, almost always, a cheaper version of their typical high-quality features. This has some merit in meeting the market price issues, but is likely genuine in that some clients only desire the "Timber-Look" in just the great room or kitchen and thus not as rustic everywhere. Note that the usual case for these hybrid marketed homes is that they are usually much larger than our last home sizes. The greater floor area that is not timber-like reverts back to conventional construction techniques. Our version of using hybrid building techniques means that we are using variations in the basic SIP technology to improve our building process, not just cheapen it.

Another key factor in our market is important to the building Green issues. That is, the closeness of the available product. If you spend a huge amount of energy transporting the raw materials, or even the finished module, to the actual building site, the shade of Green fades. Our closest supplier to North Georgia is within an hour's drive. His specialties are mainly with the EPS foam products and smaller size SIPs and roof panels. Typical sizes are 4' wide by 8' high. Roof panels can be up to 4' by 16'. Also, he has limited his fabrication capabilities for his particular market. Using a simple 4×8 panel, with the foam fabrication being the 2×6 relief zones

(1½" × 5½") on the panel perimeter and the round holes in the EPS foam for the horizontal and vertical electrical wiring chases still provides a good building module. An occasional 24"- or 30"-wide SIP also generates some flexibility.

When we match the desire to use our available SIP wall module with our Timber-Truss roof structure, we have a fairly neat mating. Interestingly, using Chalet-Style buildings results in the Timber Trusses typically spaced at 4' centers to support both the loft floor load plus the roof load. When one wants an open cathedral look, the Queen-style, decorative truss can move to 6' spacing for the roof load. (See Figure 8.2.) The eight loft trusses on the right side are at this typical plywood sheet (4×8) spacing of 4'. As you move to the far left of the building you may note the structural gap increasing to 6' for the Queen Truss about to be lifted in place

(on the ground holding frame). The 4' panels are SIPs, not just plywood sheets. Note also at this 4' juncture, a pre-cut, pre-drilled Glulam beam (3⅛" × 5½") is attached around the two mating foam relief zones to support the timber trusses. Note here that these short posts are all identical, are pre-made in the shop, and erected very quickly in the field (another good building module, only need about a dozen or so). We follow the industry guidelines for attaching these joints and sealing as Morley typically instructs. Note also that this junction point structure lends itself to more intense techniques for higher wind zones. For example, and we have used, concrete embedded metal straps that can tie into these larger posts for higher-wind tie-down resistance. Fewer, shorter and stronger SIP screws can tie this strap to the beams without using forty million nails. (Less/more.) The bottom line: this cabin

Figure 8.3 SIP roof with 4×8 exposed.

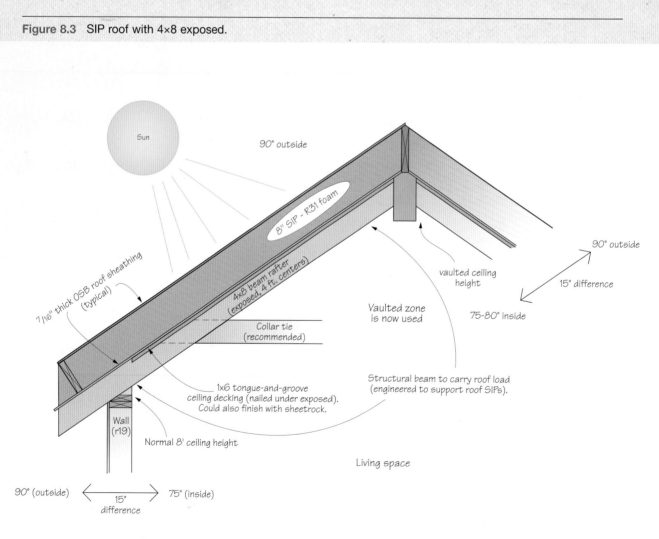

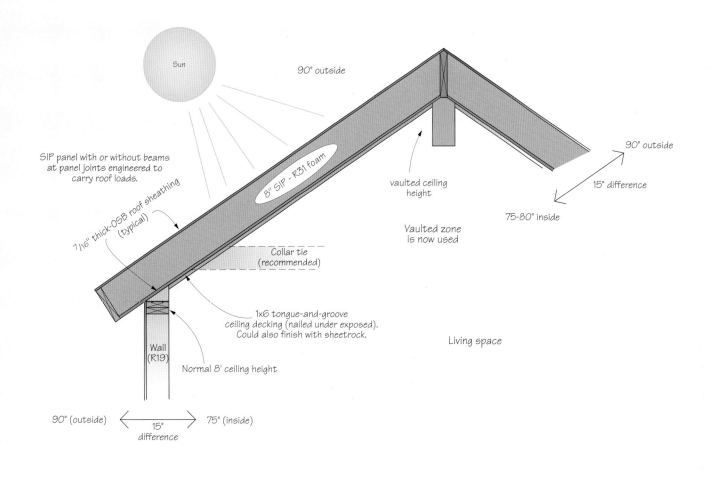

Figure 8.4 SIP roof internal structure.

project only needed a total of 20 of these smaller SIP panels for the main floor walls.

You will note a small difference in the dual window zone where the Queen truss will reside. (See Figure 8.2.) The area below the window opening is not sheaved and typical 2×6 framing is evident. A not-as-distinct clue is in the significant size of gable end wall. The size of this rough triangle also points to the amount of material required for the increase in roof pitch. This gable, matching the Timber Truss shape exactly, is simply too large for the largest SIP panels. Thus, our hybrid approach is that these two type of modules were pre-framed with conventional framing per exact drawings given to the framing crew. Also, as we experimented with cutting and modifying the standard SIP sizes, our supplier's available technology showed that the price increased dramatically and other issues arose. Part of the reasoning here is that our experience with SIPs, like any technology, has both a learning curve and tradeoff's — the natural resistance of

residential contractors willing to change their construction formulas. Special tools, techniques and training are also needed. However, we saw that the standard framing of these special modules actually made the SIP process work better. These few different zones can be spray-foam insulated later to approach the integrity of SIPs. Interestingly, most wiring tends to concentrate around these window zones. With them typically framed, the wiring access from the basement runs (using engineered floor trusses) were easily accessed. This simplification also aided the electrical sub-contractor in adjusting to this new-fangled SIP stuff. With wiring runs getting to this zone, feeding horizontally left or right to just one SIP section, via the SIP foam channels already cut, was relatively painless. Also, where wiring came directly into the existing SIP channel, we had a router tool-and-bit kit to facilitate cutting the electrical box slot. I believe we had only five or six routered electrical box locations in the entire cabin. The bottom line of this project — with

Figure 8.5   Larger SIP's for walls.

Figure 8.6   Larger SIP's — roof with ridge beam.

the 20 SIPs, the SIP-posts cut, the pre-framed window modules, the two large gable walls pre-framed, a three-man carpenter crew erected the perimeter walls in one day. For this 1450 sq. ft. cabin, the nine Timber Truss kits with the ridge beams and the two large gable end walls were lifted and erected in several hours with a boom truck the following day. The client could then cover this safe structure with tarps to preserve the integrity of his investment. Oh yes, the local builders "don't use tarps around here". However, when they did use tarps (required) in this case, they were able to work inside the next day while it was raining, and not lose a day or more of work, unlike other building sites.

Two other projects with 7 and 9 Timber Trusses, with the gable sections already in place required only about four hours of boom-truck time. Both of these project's gable-end modules, requiring them to match the Timber Truss profile, were built from the same detailed framing drawing at significantly different times and sites. My rough assessment of these two projects with the gable ends in place was that the labor time to build them in place in the air

would cost more than pre-building them as a modules and using the boom-time charges. Almost all of these pre-framed modules could be pre-built in a shop environment and brought to the site for fast assembly. As these pre-framed modules become more standardized efficiency improves dramatically. This validates why the so-called "custom" home is not so good. In the EnergyStar House chapter, we detail more techniques that these hybrid steps will yield.

On a broader range of cosmetic tastes, beyond our wood beam look, SIPs can fit this conventional style well. Figure 8.3 shows the adaptation of a SIP roof system similar to the basic exposed wood beam. With the idea that the surface finish is dictating the appearance and not the structural wood beam supporting the SIP, sheetrock or other plaster-like texture, with proper rules utilized, will allow a wider range of wall and ceiling finishes.

Even though SIPs have tremendous structural strength, at some intermediate distances of spanning, some other structural beams will likely be needed. For example, a large ridge beam with SIPs spanning from the eave wall to the ridge and some hidden internal beams at the SIP joints will provide this look. Figure 8.4 shows one version of this style. The large ridge beam may also be an engineered structural beam product like LVLs. The LVL surface can be covered with a painted or even wood-look trim finish. Also, a mixture of just a few supporting mid-size rafter beams, or purlins of exposed wood, mixed with the formal paint finish on the sheetrock will achieve an intermediate appearance. This set of formal styles,

and our more preferred rustic Timber approach, validates the flexibility of the SIP technology.

With the aid of a SIP manufacturer's pictures we can explore some buildings using the SIP structure concept drawings just discussed. Figure 8.5 shows that larger SIPs can provide for more conventional, non-timber type homes. With the larger SIP units shown, the speed and size of construction is quick. Note how clean the site appears. There is not much scrap wood to clean up and deliver to a dump. The scrap pieces simply do not exist — only the larger panel modules pre-cut before arriving at the site.

Figure 8.6 shows the large roof SIPs being installed on a large supporting ridge beam. With the embedded 2× on the SIP perimeter and the central load-carrying ability of the large ridge beam, the roof weight is properly supported. This cosmetic approach fits a more conventional interior finish (sheetrock, painted colors, etc.), not the softer, more wood-like, Timber-Style. (The green on the SIPs is a manufacturer-applied moisture protection.)

Figure 8.7   Large SIP roof with ridge and purlins.

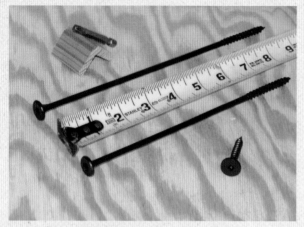

Figure 8.8 SIP screws.

Figure 8.9 SIP corner showing panel screws.

Figure 8.7 shows that bigger SIPs can be used to create even larger structures. In the left side of the picture is a timber-like post-and-beam with horizontal purlins carrying part of the roof load, which is apparently desired by the client for this area. The right side will be more "conventional" in finish, with no exposed wood beams. Observe the size and complexity of the roof panels in the foreground compared to the minimal about of fabrication work that doesn't have to be done in the field. This project also shows the blending of styles.

Using these SIPs, one can see a pattern confirming one of our expressed fundamentals: less is more. Less large panels means less scrap wood pieces sprayed out over the building site's landscape. Also, we don't need a million or so small

nails being air-driven and pulverizing our desired assembly. We use just a few, larger, stronger SIP screws. These high-strength, self drilling marvels are shown in Figure 8.8. Using high-grade steel and narrow shaft diameters means no pre-drilling. A carpenter's battery-powered drill is all that is necessary for installation — only seconds per screw. The driver bit shown is a new Spider pattern that is easier to use than the original No.3 square drive. Technology sometimes reaches down to this level.

These panel screws are strong, with shear and pullout in the 500-600 pound range so that as few as eight will provide about two tons of strength *at each corner* of the home.

Figure 8.9 shows a sample SIP corner using several of these panel screws to tie the two walls together. This is one reason why SIP homes hold up well in high-wind environments. Think back when I talked about conventional vented roofs that just have 7/16" OSB and 1/2" sheetrock protecting you overhead. Think how resistant the roof panel in Figure 8.6 will be to wind and debris damage with two layers of OSB sandwiching thick, impact-absorbing EPS foam attached with these monster screws. (Texas Tech has already tested these panel styles at hurricane levels).

A sheetrock sub-contractor, after installing the sheetrock in one of our SIP projects, said, "I don't see walls as square and straight as these anymore". So again, our less/more strategy nets better quality. Cutting and nailing thousands of little wood pieces together to make a custom house will not ensure it is a quality one — it just has a customized label for you to feel good about (or think you feel good).

In Figure 8.9, you can see that the panels fit tightly together. This means low energy usage. In our discussion about insulating the corner T's with conventional framing walls as shown in Figure 6.4, we required an extra fabrication step or two with more material (special cut foam pieces) to achieve a low-energy, or tighter sealing corner, in that construction style. With the SIP corner, only a single 2×6 fills the end of the panel. Simply caulking the inside prior to inserting the 2×6 and nailing with a smaller nail (No.8 or No.10) on both OSB sides achieves this same goal, yet much simpler. In fact, since there is only one 2×6 on each end of the two overlapping SIP modules, a higher R-value corner results since there is less wood (lower R value than the EPS foam insulating barrier). The typically 8"-long SIP screw goes through the double OSB layers and into the opposite wall's end 2×6. (With caulking on the inner OSB surface faced against the other wall's end 2×6.) That holding force by the panel screws also clamps the caulked joint tighter than the best air-nailer. We now have an air-tight corner in addition to a strong one.

How tight is this corner and the other SIP construction methods discussed? The United States EPA division is now *not* requiring the door blower test on SIP homes. The last several years of testing SIP homes to meet the EnergyStar ACH (Air Exchange) leakage minimum of .35 ACH have been exceeded. This EPA formal certification is a true and accurate measure of quality.

A validation of lower SIP framing labor costs was reported in a March 2008 newsletter by the NHAB (www.nbnnews.com). This article related that a study done by the BASF Corporation on a two-story, three bedroom SIP home in Tifton, New Jersey, demonstrated that framing costs could be cut about in half over conventional "stick-built". And, I think our simplified, single-floor concept is one step better. This decrease in labor should offset higher material costs of SIPs. A recent project of mine, a small 500 sq. ft. guest house, shows how a client's decisions can be muddled with bad information. In this case, the framer's quoted labor for the main floor was the same for framing with conventional 2×6s or for erecting the pre-made SIP walls. The entire SIP exterior wall concept totaled eight panels: Two eave-sided, 8'-high by 23'-wide sections and three vertical 7-8'-wide SIPs each per gable end in a balloon style (for vaulted ceiling height above an 8' eave). My estimate for erecting the eight SIPs and the three Timber Trusses was about eight hours of boom-truck time and two carpenters (one a helper grade) for the same period. This SIP-erecting labor cost should be less than a four-man crew taking more than a day or two to frame and sheave these walls. Also, the Timber Trusses would be installed as well as the R40/R24 combination walls already insulated (at a higher grade level than the R19 spray-foam). The client *thought* the SIP costs were higher than they actually were. The SIP supplier, capable of manufacturing these large size panels, was located farther away than our normal small panel supplier. This 480-mile distance would barely make the LEED local distance goal. Obviously the increased shipping charges as well as the cost per panel, with only eight panels, factored into the final cost. I have two concerns demonstrated by this example: First, the client's end product, although very good, could have been better for about 2-3% more real cost increase of the entire project. And second, I suggest that contractors and sub-contractors, resisting proven building technologies like SIPs, should heed names like Studebaker, Plymouth, or more recently, Oldsmobile. These product names no longer exist because they did not adapt when their markets changed.

SIPs have great potential for our last-home market. In addition to the structural improvements, the confirmed energy savings and the speed of erection at the site, SIPs are a proven product. Despite requiring more planning and shop drawings, SIPs lend themselves to gained productivity if the sizes of the modules were standardized. The safety of SIP construction has been demonstrated by the tornado wind levels tests shown in Morley's IPS book on page 11 in Clermont, Georgia. Compare this to the 2×4 studded, OSB braced-corners-only houses in the nearby county that were blown-apart. As our current search for oil alternatives evolves, I hope we also will develop more bio-diesel-like fuels that will aid in making insulating foams of higher R-values.

In the end, if we strive to design and build smarter and rational-sized homes, SIP technology will be a key building block.

> I suggest that contractors and sub-contractors, resisting proven building technologies like SIPs, should heed names like Studebaker, Plymouth, or more recently, Oldsmobile.

A Practical Dose of Passive Solar

Gaining even a fragment of the sun's energy into your home has been a lure for eons. But achieving a practical  method of obtaining this energy is the challenge. The building's orientation, layout and general design is critical for maximizing southern exposure (In North America). Many homes can gain some energy benefits by applying a few passive-solar design techniques. There is some confusion between passive solar and active solar, so a brief orientation of these two different and possibly overlapping concepts will help you understand which methods can work for you.

Passive solar means the house alone was designed to maximize the ability of the house to gain sun energy. This means that you should select the best building site where most of the windows are on the south elevation and as few windows as possible on the north and west sides and a few windows on the east. These window locations are a challenge when the designer's focus is only on curb-appeal. Many of the concepts discussed to this point for a last home are also important for a passive solar home being successful. The house does not have to be weird or futuristic in design. However, the cosmetic design penalties discussed earlier will compound the challenges in meeting this goal.

ACTIVE SOLAR

In order to achieve a successful active-solar home, you generally need to have the basics of a passive-

solar home. Active-solar adds some sophisticated and somewhat expensive technology to the home. Two main components are typical: PV (Photo-Voltaic) cells and water heating panels (hot-water use). The PV cells generate low-voltage DC (direct current) energy that needs to be converted to AC (alternating current) household voltage with electrical modules called *inverters*. However, with high-tech progression, the PV cells are getting more efficient and cost effective. Hot water heating sub-systems for domestic use are also improving. My recommendation for active solar is, if you are achieving most of the goals we have outlined in general and you are obtaining passive-solar

Figure 9.1 Seasonal sun position on south facing windows.

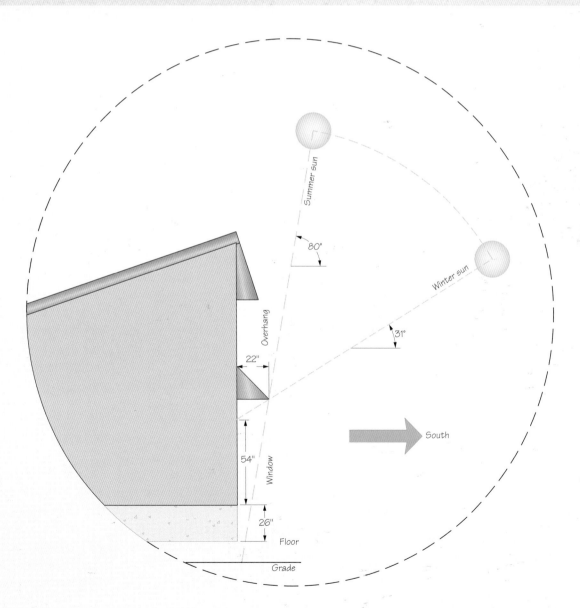

capability, investment in solar hot water heating, even as boost for the main hot water energy source, is a good choice. The next step would be some PV cells for lighting or emergency lighting, for example, DC LED lamps. If you have downsized significantly, achieved the goals outlined, still have some resources and desire to go "off the grid" even more, go for it. There are many technical sources and Web sites that will help you learn more about active solar.

Figure 6.1 has a wedge shape on the attached garage roof. The vertical face on the south-facing side was intended for future solar panels. We now have a standard Timber Truss module for those who want to go solar. Several passive-solar homes have also used this universal shape. Many years ago, we had a working electronic control system for hot air that was tested for years. As noted in my daughter's college fund story, the house worked so well with the passive solar techniques, the hot air control wasn't needed. The current owner could easily add either PV cells or hot water heating panels in this zone.

PASSIVE SOLAR

More passive solar techniques that may be employed in your future home are talked about in Mazria's Passive Solar Book. Figure 9.1 shows the fundamental solar concepts for a North Georgia home. Note that the main window wall is facing almost due south. (The building site will probably pose some limitations as to the positioning of the house.) The earth's rotation changes the angle of the sun through the seasons. The angles shown are at noon at the high point (June 21) and low point (December 21) of the sun in North Georgia. Regional differences are found in the book referenced. These angle changes provide the differences in energy delivered by the sun, similar to the changes as one travels closer to the equator and notices it getting warmer. The angle change is the key to making the passive solar work.

This occurs only on the south side of the house. I believe most of us want more heat and light coming in the house during the colder months and, if possible, none in the warmer months. (Maybe a little in the spring and fall months.) Figure 9.2 shows how far the sun will penetrate into the home during the winter low point. The sun warmth at this colder time of the year is generally welcomed.

Figure 9.2 Sun penetration in Winter.

Mother nature will help us if we are diligent and understand her rules! If you have placed most of your windows on the south elevation, make the sizing trade off of the windows and have the overhang over them, you can capture this energy at the right time of the year. The overhang ratio and the window height down is about a 1-to-3 ratio. This F-factor can be calculated for each region using Mazria's book. Now, going horizontal, with a rectangular shaped house, wider windows and having one floor begins to make sense. A tall window on the main level is more challenging. With a second floor, you must do the same overhang technique on the windows independent of the first floor. Tall, French patio doors with glass and full-glass sliding doors (less/more), with their great view of the deck railings, are also a challenge. So called passive-solar homes, shown in magazines, with huge two-story glass and improper overhangs aren't truly effective.

Before we explore the north, east and west sides of the home, remember that the preferred home design is one main floor plus a basement. Basement windows will have the same shading needs. A simple framed structure for those desiring active PV or hot-water panels in this overhang is a creative solution. Not only are the utility connections likely closer, the mounted angle can be optimized for the region and the window overhang shading solution solved. Also, the panels are less obvious at this basement level and some neighborhood cosmetic architectural issues may be solved.

Using the earlier 150 sq. ft. horizontal window wall example, let's see how much sun energy we get in these windows in late December to January in our region. We will receive about 1,500 BTUs per square foot of window per solar day. (A solar day is 9:30AM to 3:30PM — six hours average.) This window group will bring about 225,000 BTUs into the house. If you properly saved and stored this energy and doled it out over the next 24 hours, you would have 9,400 BTUs per hour for free. Since most of us have heard of "tons" relating to air conditioners and heat pumps, let's convert to that figure (12,000 BTU/hour = ton). Thus, we have about 3/4 ton of heat pump value coming to you from just this set of windows. In our North Georgia climate, well-built houses typically need heat pumps from 2½- to 4-ton sizes.

Ten years of testing of our little mountain cabin (1,250 sq. ft. on the main level) yielded some interesting results. Our calculated heat load is around 15,000 BTUs per hour. We have a 1.5 ton heat pump, which is about 18,000 BTU/hour. On sunny cold days (20-40°F), our house frequently has long periods during the day when our heat pump does not need to turn on. Our comfort level (68-72° without heat pump), exceeds our neighbor's reported figures. I only have one window on the north and one window on the west (my office den, for view, with hardwood-tree shading in the warm months).

If one of the windows from the south wall was moved to the north wall, not only would you lose the winter sun gain, the energy loss from the north would be significant. Moving this one window is worth about 1/12 ton. If you moved it to the east wall, you would have some unwanted gain in the summer morning sun which isn't too bad. If you moved it to the west wall, the sun would shine in for long periods. Mother nature always wins, you just pay the monthly energy bill for her efforts.

In the warmer climates, the SHGC (solar heat gain coefficient) rating on the window is more important. A higher SHGC value can minimize extra heat gain in warmer periods.

Now that we have this energy gain from the sun controlled in the house, here's the second-half of the design: *Thermal mass.* We need to have enough high-density material (like masonry) in our homes area to absorb sun energy and average its effects out over time. The thermal density of the average home's interior is not enough capacitance. A general rule of thumb is about 8 to 9 sq. ft. of 4-5"-thick concrete floor slab per square foot of the south window area. Using our 150 sq. ft. set of windows, we need about 1,200 sq. ft. of concrete flooring. This seems like a lot. The basement concrete is disconnected from the main floor, but is some help in dispersing extra heat gain. Radiant heated floors can provide a comfortable environment. Modern versions work well with hardwood floors, but they don't have enough mass for our needs. The simplest slab-floor solution uses ceramic floor coverings or decorative concrete designs for those wanting that appearance. If you have a lot of stone already planned around your fireplace's vertical wall area and major dividing side walls stone covered, these will add to the thermal mass. Our passive-solar mountain cabin has a thinner concrete walls with stone veneer finish on the interior side walls of the great room. On the other side of each wall is a bedroom with a different style and color of stone. This was our preferred tastes. If you want to explore some unique concepts like Trombe Walls, water walls, etc., you can refer to the *Passive Solar Book*, but remember, our guideline is to always keep things simple.

If we have the proper south windows, the proper overhang, and a fair amount of slab floor space with radiant heating, knowing the typical sun area covered inside is useful. For an average depth house (24'-26' deep), the sun path in mid-day summer is outside the window. At mid-day in winter,

> We receive about 1,500 BTUs per square foot of window per solar day. That means 150 sq. ft. of windows will bring about 225,000 BTUs into the house.

the sun path will cover about half of the floor. The south and north floor slabs can have different radiant heating parameters and controls. If you have the zone control capability, the north floor zone can be "on" more than the south zone to equalize comfort for the radiant heating. (The maximum utilization of the thermal mass is better in the southern half of the floor.) If other floor coverings are desired in the rear floors, they don't have to be slab. There are structural issues that have to be designed for each case. One of our conceptual projects on the horizon, the "Jetson's" house, will likely use the above techniques because the client wants a more fire-resistant and safe room environment. They will gain several things by investing in these techniques.

One passive-solar technique for homes not able to maximize this gain in the main house is an *attached* sun room. This addition, 8-12' deep and about 20' wide, can be designed to mesh into a variety of architectural situations. It needs to follow the south-facing, thermal mass and shading rules. This addition has an advantage over a classic screened-in porch. If you utilize some adjustable shading concepts, like manual or electrically controlled roll-up awnings, you can control the problem of shading the house in the summer. With the awning rolled up, this is a better winter space than the unusable porch. Planting hobbies, etc, also benefit during this colder period. During the warm months, the awning is covering the top and overhang. By planning to dump the extra heat gain directly into the adjacent room, say a great room or a dining room, passive solar energy gain is achieved. This sunroom addition can work on a lot not generally enabling passive solar gain for the main house. Two-story versions of sunrooms are also available.

GREENHOUSE AND SUNROOM

If the site permits only the greenhouse approach and doesn't have a main elevation facing south, and assuming there is a sloping lot/basement scenario, an earth-retaining wall, preferably poured concrete, is needed. The shape and design of this bermed wall will contribute to the thermal mass needed. If you are able to incorporate some insulating techniques behind the wall against the earth, this mass value is improved. This also removes one of the side-wall costs of the sunroom, since this earth-retaining/berm wall covers this area. A variation

of this approach can be used in a full-south-wall approach or if the house doesn't face directly south.

A sunroom works well when it is attached to the daylight basement portion and is connected to the window/airflow scheme on the main level as shown in Figure 9.3.

The airflow operation of this location mates so well with main-level-only-plus-basement layouts. We noted earlier how increased building height makes the air temperature harder to control in two-story homes. By generating this warmer air at the basement level, it works well. The basement area is slightly cooler than the main level, so the heat rises to where it's needed. The sunroom roof overlap height over the basement is just below the windows of the main level. (See Figure 9.3.) Adding 12-16"-tall awning windows under the main windows provides heat gain control for the main level. These lower awning windows will be opened during the sunny winter days and closed at night. The warm air will flow into the sunroom and into the main-level room above. This sunroom would be located on a south wall where a porch/deck is not planned for the main level. By dumping the warm air during the winter days, the thermal-mass effect of the sunroom is still working to store the excess heat not drained off to the main floor room.

This sunroom shows that even *some* solar gain for part of the home is beneficial. The upcoming "Jetson's" house doesn't face the ideal southeast orientation. However, this larger-than-average-house has three modules that are 24', 48', and 24' wide, joined at 120° angles to form a courtyard. One 24' wing does face almost due south. Our current plan shows this room to be an office. Since the clients work at home, this works in their favor. We don't plan to put a deck here because the other two modules provide enough deck space. By adding a sunroom in front of, and below the office at the basement level, they have a terrific mountain view out their office windows. During winter days the lower awning windows will provide a substantial amount of daytime heating. (In Figure 6.1, the attached sunroom frequently generated temperatures of 95-100° inside on sunny and cold winter days. This is ¾ ton of heating.) Since the office will use this energy during daylight hours, the balance will be absorbed in the thermal mass of the greenhouse floor and will dissipate to the cooler basement after

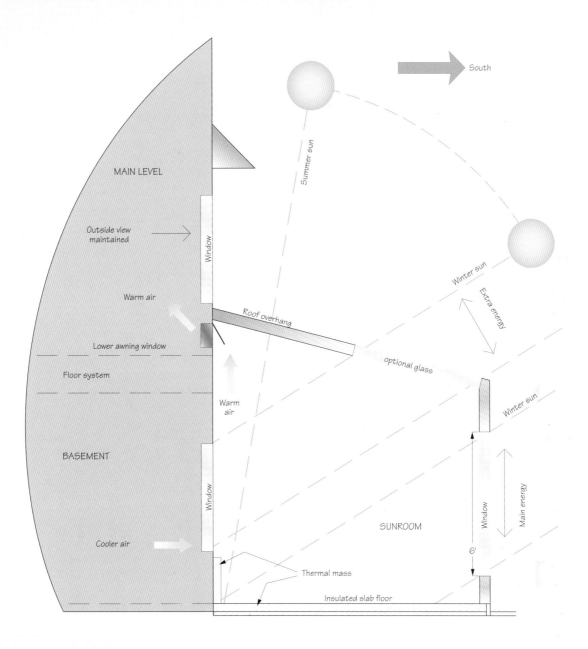

Figure 9.3 Attached sunroom in basement.

daylight hours. This passive solar energy stuff is neat — and it works!

The optional roof glass area below the solid roof overhang section is additional solar energy not accounted for in the numbers just presented. With this combination of solid overhang and partial glass, you are applying the proper overhang for the basement level window. This means that the light energy that makes it through the sunroom glass and inside the basement, providing heat gain. The excess glass and its resulting energy will offset the energy portion used for the main level office space during the daylight hours. There are two thermal-mass zones: The insulated concrete slab floor and stone or brick below the basement window. The energy stored in this thermal mass will continue to assist the basement and at minimum, provide an intermediate temperature buffer to the colder outside air. Even more free energy is available!

The sunroom example in Figure 9.3 combines passive and active solar concepts. With the attached sunroom, the roof sections become optimal places to locate solar panels, either PV or hot-water-only heating panels. Increasing the roof pitch of the front wall of the sunroom will optimize the winter-sun angle. The view side of the simplified floor

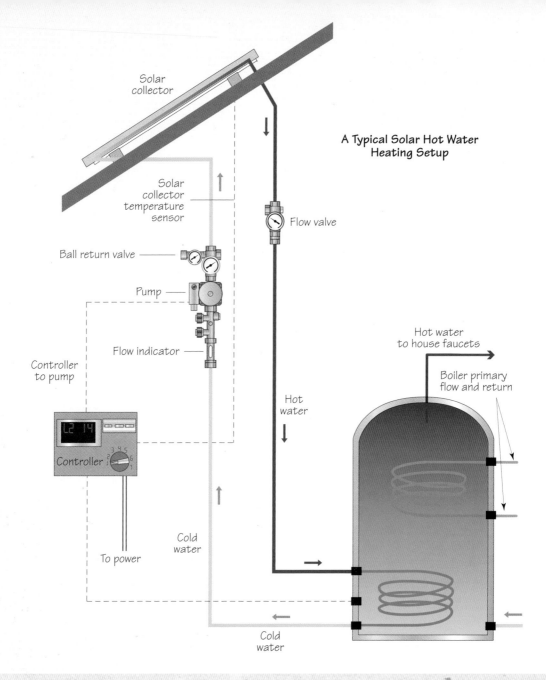

Solar
collector

Solar
collector
temperature
sensor

Ball return valve

Pump

Flow indicator

Controller
to pump

Controller

To power

Cold
water

A Typical Solar Hot Water
Heating Setup

Flow valve

Hot
water

Cold
water

Hot water
to house faucets

Boiler primary
flow and return

Cold
water

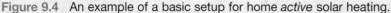

Figure 9.4 An example of a basic setup for home *active* solar heating.

plan (see Figure 5.2) is generally away from the street (or curb-appeal side). (Assuming that one chose the building lot for passive-solar orientation first.) The active solar panels are now close to the location of the home's utilities, such as HVAC, hot water heater, etc. and not on the main level of the home. The passive solar sunroom facilitates the active panels by providing a stable, non-freezing environment to connect to these active elements to the main utilities. Even with solar energy concepts, less can net more.

This attached sunroom was a popular passive-solar technique in the late 1970s to 1980s and is still is a proven concept to be considered as one of our future energy-cost-savings solution.

Thus, passive-solar techniques should be considered a tie-breaker for trading off curb-appeal choices when planning a final home. If no view or other factor dictates the way the house points, picking up passive solar energy helps in swinging the choice to face south. The relative position of key rooms within this footprint, or even less south-facing lots may optimize that room's value. Within a room, the selection of not only window location, but size now can yield better results. The sunroom idea, implemented with or without a screened porch, can be a major payback.

10

Who Really Likes Repainting?

A little painting project can be fun but a life-long painting of a home's exterior features is reminiscent of the San Francisco Golden Gate Bridge — the painting crew starts at one end and works to the other end and then starts over again. Is  this fun or torture? In one development, the painting contractor never has to leave his mountain location. He simply books painting and staining jobs for all the little cabins that constantly need work. He is so busy on this repair painting work that it has been difficult to obtain his services for new construction projects. He has generated an East Coast microcosm of the Golden Gate Bridge's painting crew's routine.

My particular interest in sustainability and low-maintenance exterior products comes from three sources.

First my personal experiences range from my homes and remodeling projects to many friend's projects that I have assisted with. Second, I have several professional associates that specialize in remodeling only, not new construction. Those remodeling experiences reveal more than building a new house in terms of tracking or knowing the problems that arise in older homes. These remodeling guys see the long-term issues and mistakes in the battlefield, not the bubbly sales person in the new model home. My third source is our annual GRASP community service project. My daughter "drafted me" with the winning phrase: "Dad, can you help out a little at our church youth group's project?" Several years of managing the construction portion of this wonderful service activity resulted from those words. Her group, with adult leaders heading teams of youths, work for three days aiding elderly clients. The work ranges from landscaping and cleanup tasks to several deck/stair repairs. We focus on safety assistance like wheelchair ramps and safe access to and from the home. Since one of my key tasks is evaluating, months in advance, potential client sites for projects we can safely accomplish with the youth (and adult leader support) I see a number of extreme and sad cases. Those cases remind me of about the falling-person story — when they finally do hit the ground. Then it's too late!

What may first appear as a contradiction about soft touch of warm wood on the interior is actually a pointer to the entire home buying/planning choice. Here's a clue from Mother Nature: Wood appears outside in the natural world — with one key ingredient — bark. Wood does not exist very long without bark protecting it. The process of choosing this rustic-wood approach is usually done without thinking it through. Here's my advice: Avoid wood on the *exterior* of your home like a plague.

I realize that wood suppliers will react to this statement and counter with data, marketing efforts, focus group's, etc. Use this special warm product judiciously inside the home. It is not a Green material if it's used outside and it rots — this is not what *sustainable* means. Where are you spending your time? Use this wonderful product where you will enjoy its warmth.

Don't use wood doors for the exterior, not even in protected areas such as a covered-porch entry. The money spent here can be invested in higher grade, solid wood doors for the interior. In fact this is a perfect application of my dreaded French doors on the exterior. Utilize the beautiful wood version inside for an office, den or library. The average wood exterior door has an insulation value of R1. Those wood panel sidelights have the same problem. This means that the door looses as much energy as almost the entire wall (assuming a minimum of R19) that it is located in. And this assumes that it has low-infiltration seals, which likely it will not. I suggest using either a steel-frame (preferred) or fiberglass, foam-filled (EnergyStar rated) door. These doors are R6 to R8 and generally have better sealing characteristics, plus more low-maintenance options for the frame. For example, aluminum clad trim and non-rotting, adjustable thresholds are available. If you desire some glass in this high-insulation door, many nice stained glass or decorative options exist, still energy-efficient, particularly if you are prudent to keep the glass area less than half of the door's full area. As a contrast to this exterior door, look at the French doors in Figure 10.1. This is where wood doors (and windows) belong, inside the home in a beautiful wood-trimmed library, not outside decaying. Get more with less. You will appreciate the wood interior door daily and not have to worry about painting or eventually replacing the exterior door.

Masonry products are the first-choice in sustainable products. First, brick is an excellent starting point but due to its formal nature, it doesn't always fit more casual environments. However, there are a few product lines that should be considered because they look rustic. E.Dillon has a line of brick, with different sizes available, that looks like European stone. ALBA has a similar product. Bricks range from $2-$3.50/sq. ft. The unique stone-like cost a little more. Brick mason labor charges in our region range from $3-$4/sq. ft. The total cost per sq. ft. ranges from $5-$8/sq. ft.. A technical requirement for brick is that you need a brick ledge, effectively a small footing width extension in the foundation. These cost and design issues need to be factored in. Some developments may not allow brick. A mix-and-match of brick and stone is another choice.

There are two types of stone: Natural stone and synthetic or cultured stone, which is man-made. I prefer any stone on the exterior to be natural and

Figure 10.1   Interior French doors.

Figure 10.2   Brick and stone combination.

Figure 10.3 Garage stone corner and stucco wall.

Figure 10.4 Gable-end cement-based shingles.

cultured stone in the interior. The advantage of cultured stone is that it is light weight and does not require extra structural costs. Natural stone can be used two ways: Stacked or veneered. Stacked, like the attractive "dry-stacked" type is more horizontal and requires more material for coverage. Stacked stone may cover only twenty to forty square feet out of a ton of stone. The costs range from $6-$10/sq. ft. and the labor is higher, about $8-$12/sq. ft. So, the stacked total costs range from $14-$20/sq. ft. Obviously these estimates are time and region related.

The veneered style, locally called "stick-on" up here in the mountains, is flatter and uses less material. Typically stick-on will yield 100-140 sq. ft. per ton, depending on material thickness. Veneered is structurally simpler and rarely needs a brick-ledge footing (it "sticks" right on the vertical wall, with wire mesh and mortar, and no base support is needed). Material costs range from $1-$2/foot for thicker, bolder-looking stone. Labor rates are about $5-$8/sq. ft.

Another choice for exterior masonry is hard stucco, which is concrete-based. However, in a cost-sensitive application such as a garage or covering concrete erosion control walls, a simple stucco layer can be less than $2/sq. ft. The higher grade stucco is $4-$6/sq. ft.

Wood siding exteriors include pine lapped or chink-like sidings cost $1/sq. ft. for the lesser-grade pine while Douglas Fir and cedar will cost $2-$4/sq. ft. The log-sided shaped, typically lesser-grade pine is $3/sq. ft. This is due to its larger thickness, with the milling to mimic the "D" shape of a log home exterior.

Remember that this exterior wood siding will need re-staining in the future. The average stain on wood-sided cabins does not seem to last as long as a paint on a more formal wood house. (A respected paint store owner shared with me: "Stain is just watered down paint".) The average re-stain job lasts about 2-4 years and costs about $3,500-$4,500. With these typical cabins having around 1,600-1,700 sq. ft. of exterior area to cover, there is a recurring cost at least $2 per foot.

Let's use a simple case for a typical "weekender" house of brick instead of wood. The wood's initial cost is about $5,000. The brick version would be about $11,000-$12,000. With two re-stains over the next few years, the brick will have paid for itself. Note that veneered stone would also be in the cost range of brick. I am not suggesting, nor prefer myself, that an all-stone or all-brick house is a choice for all. (This design process is just beginning. The stacked stone is starting to look like Frank Lloyd Wright's Falling Water house.)

Even with solid masonry products and using high-grade windows, allow for trim width around the windows and within the masonry opening. This trim, a low-maintenance type, will enable easier window replacement without tearing into the costly masonry.

Let's look at mixing and matching some masonry styles. Figure 10.2 shows that one can, if careful, use both brick and stone. Figure 11.2 shows a garage bermed wall. As we move around the side of this garage, as shown in Figure 10.3, this side, since it's not on the side facing the street, uses a low cost application of stucco, which is applied on the concrete wall. The stone only wraps around the corner for about 16-20". This column wrap corner, on a garage or on the main house (using a higher-grade hard stucco), opens up more options without using stone over the entire house. This technique can also be used with brick (or even stone-looking brick) mixed with stucco. Stacked-stone is another option but it is more expensive. The stacked stone can be put just below the windows (with reasonable-height windows) and the stucco used for the bulk of the wall above the stone base. A sustainable variation is that the natural stone is more resistant to the effects of water splash near the ground than either stucco or wood.

For example, if we covered a 9'-high by 26'-wide exterior wall (234 sq. ft.) in veneered stone, it would cost about $1,600, if covered in stucco, it would cost about $900 and if covered in wood, it would cost about $700 (the first time only). If we have 18"-wide veneer stone wrap columns at the two corners: and stucco over the bulk of the surface, our total cost is about $1,000. Practicality and having an attractive exterior can work together.

CEMENT-BASED PRODUCTS

Other sustainable exterior products are cement-based. Unlike wood, they won't rot and are unlikely to have a replacement-cost issue. One of the most recognized names for this line is James Hardie. The basic product is lap siding, in long lengths so that the upper layer *laps* over the lower one. The

Figure 10.5 Gable-end cement board-and-batten.

Cement trim is available, but the cement dust creating when cutting the thicker 1× trim is a health issue. (Thinner panel products can be cut with shears.) I suggest a composite trim called Miratec. It is not cement based, but it is still low-maintenance and will not rot. It has a wood-textured look that works with the cement siding and shingles.

Figures 10.4 shows cement panels on the lower portion of a wall using Miratec trim at 16" spacings for a traditional board-and-batten look. This has a material cost of a few dollars per square foot. The gable above the main floor shows staggered shingles that make a nice trim that is practical and sustainable. This shingle material cost is in the $4/sq. ft. range. Painting costs need to be added to the cement product, and the detailed labor to make angle cuts can add up. But the wider sheets of the cement shingles are faster to install than smaller shingles. Figure 10.5 shows a building end where the gable end is not seen from the street. In this case we continued the board-and-batten look on the gable end with a better cost result. For an even lower cost, the panels could have trim at the 2' to 4' spacings.

One "penny-wise/dollar-foolish" thing that happens is not using stainless steel nails and instead using galvanized nails. Even good galvanized nails will lose their finish over time and rust stains show up, spoiling a nice paint job. The extra cost for using stainless nails vs. galvanized is about $100 for an average home. Also, when wood siding is used, the rusty nail situation shows up even faster.

Two styles that works together are the stone on the lower part of the wall and the cement products on the larger, upper part of the wall. Regional stone variations, for the base stone, from Colorado to New England encourage the use of local materials. A third version that covers the entire wall, utilizing the basic panel product, or lap siding, with minimal trim, reduces the area needing painting.

My earlier analogy about the roof's importance to the overall house structure reminds me of advice I was seeking years ago. When I began racing sports cars, I asked an experienced friend about a recommendation for a good safety helmet. His question back to me applies here: "Just whose head are you protecting?" (Good helmets cost more money.)

I have two preferred types of long-life roof coverings: Concrete tile (or the Spanish clay-tile version) or standing-seam metal roofs. There are more and

siding is attached with stainless nails. Panel-sized products are available in 4'×8', 4'×9' and 4'×10' sizes, just like plywood. Patterns range from a wood-grain look to an embossed simulated-board/batten pattern at a 12" spacing. Concrete shingles can look like wood cedar shingles and are also available in 4'-wide strips. Shingle can have straight ends or staggered ends, which open up lots of options. These cement products do require some painting, but there are two, key finish factors. First, primer base is usually on the concrete, ready for painting. Second, since you are using paint, not stain, the finish will last longer. My field observations show that, even with mid-level paints, the paint will last eight to ten years. Longer-life paints are available. The shingles are available in a few factory-applied colors but more will most likely be available in the near future. The shingles' costs range from $3-$4/sq. ft. The panel products are about $1/sq. ft.. The painting costs $1-$2/sq. ft..

more recycle-based products available, but I want to concentrate on these two. I particularly like the fire resistance of both materials.

Roofing Materials

Roof coverings are generally marketed in a regional array of styles and colors, which aid in adaptation. I have seen them from California to South Florida as well as in Texas and Atlanta suburbs. Two suppliers that I have some reference for are Monier Tile and Hanson. Roofing experts attest to their life-long character. The code's minimum issue now appears. Some of you may be suspecting that a typically framed roof may not be up to the task. These concrete products weight about 10 pounds/sq. ft. This is much more than asphalt shingles. The higher-grade structural styles like Timber Beams and heavier SIP designs are readily able to handle this increased load. In fact, our Timber Trusses have this safety factor included. This is similar to northern climates having heavier snow-load ratings. The material cost for these shingles is not high. It's close to that of mid-grade asphalt shingles. The real cost is in labor, finding local experience, concrete cutting saws; plus other associated material costs. The weight has some transportation costs unique to the product. Occasionally shingles will crack from improper walking on them, but repair is easy. I have repaired just a few in ten years. Both the concrete versions and the Spanish versions will blend with a range of the masonry siding materials already discussed. With everything factored in, the cost averages about one-and-one-half to two times that of good asphalt shingles. And, they last at least *four times* as long.

A low-pitched roof shingled in one of these tiles is more visually appealing than the elaborate, steep-pitched, cheap-shingled roofs now prevalent in suburbia. The actual roof costs are closer than one is initially "advised" by the local experts.

Now one roof covering that I recommend is standing-seam metal. The increased cost over the generic steel roof panels seems out of line. I know the material-cost ratios of the thicker steel panels, the typical manufacturing costs, of each type, etc. But I suspect that the principal commercial market use of this product keeps the suppliers happy. I think that if the suppliers marketed a more realistic cost than the generic metal roofing (where exposed screws/washers are required), a strong sales growth would result.

This cost-variation issue leads to the major differences in standing seam over the fastener-required generic, metal-panel residential roof. The metal roof now has exposed screws on the surface with neoprene rubber washers to attach the metal to the roof. Note that roofers for commercial applications offer a higher-grade screw with the metal cap designed to cup over the bulk of the flexible washer. This metal protection cup provides longer life for the sealing washer. I always suggest to clients if they can't go with standing seam, at least use the commercial grade fastener/washer combination.

The standing-seam name refers to the small vertical bend between metal sections (typically flat, 12-16"-wide panels) that is above the plane of the roof .(Above the place where water is running, not where the typical screws and washers are located.) The fastening clips that hold the metal panels to the roof are at the seam, hidden under the metal panels. There are metal protecting clip over both halves of this raised 90° seam. Other variations are being tested and I hope their improved productivity leads to wider acceptance.

This increase in generic metal roofs for second or third generation re-roofing of older homes also validates the asphalt shingle's life vs. the metal roof's life.

Standing seam roofs, matched with some of the masonry sidings and mix/match selections yield very attractive exteriors without going to cosmetic

> With every thing factored in, the cost of concrete shingles averages about one-and-one-half to two times that of good asphalt shingles. But they last at least four times as long.

Figure 10.6 House in a village located north of Archer's Post, Kenya. Building Green and recycling of materials, yes! However, sustainability in this climate is about 3 to 5 years. (PHOTO BY JIM STACK)

design extremes. For example, a metal roof, a hard stucco top siding and a stone base combination is an attractive, long-life solution. With the range of colors available, and with the EnergyStar-rated metal color options, many choices are available.

EXTERIOR DECKS AND PORCHES

Any low maintenance discussion is incomplete without covering outdoor living spaces such decks and porches. Even the best treated woods, with the exception of some of the exotic species, will have a limited life span. The less you treat the wood, the faster Mother Nature will gain the advantage, and even the appearance, prior to wood rot will be an issue. Invest in a synthetic decking such as TREX

or EverGrain. Many test reports and reviews are available on the Internet and respected magazines like *Fine Homebuilding*. The first advice that one gets is something like, "the deck will cost twice as much". It is true that the price range of these sustainable decking products is at least two times that of pressure-treated wood. Can you accept that these will last at least twice as long (actually much longer)? The framing material is about 40% of the cost (structural 2×8 pressure-treated joists, etc), the decking covering is about 40% and the railings are about 20%. The complexity of railings, structural issues to ground height and bracing needs will adjust these three areas, but this estimate is sound. If you double the decking you are only doubling

40% for just the decking. The desire to improve the railing subsystem life will also increase the complete deck cost. But both don't double the cost.

A design element we use for some railings, if accepted by the client's tastes, and now with some local codes allowing it, is the use of a synthetic lattice pattern between the structural railing pieces. (The code issue was that railings more than 30" off the ground should not have any horizontal openings for a child to place a foot to easily facilitate climbing the railing.) There is a range of styles, patterns and colors available to blend with many of the synthetic decking and structural post' colors. By using the bold pieces of the decking 5/4 × 6 parts horizontally with the lattice sheet, and spanning, at a safe distance, the vertical posts, the average cost of the railing structure tones down the lattice look. This particular lattice material does not require you, using a little brush, to paint all those tiny diamonds or squares. It will not need this agonizing task. We use this lattice to safely cover a wide railing area that uses more expensive and larger structural material in our local annual GRASP community service projects. Since we are assisting with older homes, with lower porches (less than 30" off grade) and are frequently adding near-ground wheelchair ramps, we think this synthetic, no-maintenance lattice is a safer than using thirty-eight million, nailed, 2×2 pressure-treated vertical stiles.

One key deck structural issue is the attachment techniques to the house at the ledger board. Since most deck failures seem to be in this zone, don't cheapen structural points here. This ledger area is where long-life maintenance techniques pay dividends. Consider using an ice-and-watershield membrane against the house vs. the usual metal flashing or worse, builder's felt, as a moisture barrier. Moisture will penetrate from this pressure treated ledger into the house sheathing causing rot at the house sheathing (likely not see until after seven years). Another step, sometimes done, but now questioned, with structural concerns, is

a small, 1/4-1/2" gap between the ledger board and the house. This gap enables water to drain away from the deck. With the increase in space, the bolt strength is reduced. Larger bolts and/or more bolts may appease the inspectors, and your concerns, if you choose to do this. But be conservative. The point is that water will get into the darnedest places and cause future cost surprises.

One other deck design element is to consider dropping the entire deck plane one step from the door (7").

Since it is good design practice to have a small drop (1-2") with the deck sloping away from the house, just not too extreme. This lowering of the deck, coupled with the realistic-height window concept talked about earlier and the deck being in a prized "view zone", will optimize the view area out the window and minimize the view of the railing. The final point here is to weigh the safety issues of a one-step drop for elderly folks.

If, when planning a deck, a patio works (thus very near ground level) better than a deck or a patio combined with a deck, do it. You can utilize more masonry and other lower-maintenance products for a patio.

SOFFITS, FASCIA AND RAKE TRIMS

Soffits, fascia, and rake trims at the ends of houses take a severe beating from the elements. My testing has found that using the high-grade, low-maintenance products already discussed is the way to go. There are simply are no cheap solutions. (Pay me now or pay me later.)

Low-maintenance design rules apply to the interfacing of chimneys and streamlined roofs. A base guideline for the chimney location is to position it at the highest point possible on the roof. Cosmetic and floor-plan preferences can make this challenging. The emotional pull of the seasonally-used fireplace frequently wins out over other things like the entertainment area (TV and stereo) that are used daily. One technical factor that can

> Even the best treated woods, with the exception of some of the exotic species, will have a limited life span.

Figure 10.7 Another house in the same village north of Archer's Post, Kenya. The women design and build their homes. Part of this roof is made from a reed-like material gathered from the foot of a "nearby" (about a 20-mile/30-35km walk) mountain. The builder said this roof is very good and will last a long time. (PHOTO BY JIM STACK)

assist in this process is based on the *10'/2' rule*. That is, the building code guides the chimney's top point, horizontally, to be 10' away from the nearest pitched-roof section to be 2' taller. So, if you locate the chimney down at the lower eave edge (about 8-9' high), you still have the total chimney height. Another result of this eave location is that you will have this tall, skinny structure in the open, away from the house. Also, the "cricket" shape (like dormers), needed to shed water away and required above the chimney on the pitched roof, is a frequent leak point.

It is also a place where leaves and debris collect, enhancing rain-water damming and increasing the leak potential. I frequently see the chimney at the gable end of these mountain Chalets, *almost* making it to the ridge. The short gap below the ridge exhibits these cricket weaknesses. Ready for the real clincher? Steeper roof pitches make all of this

stuff worse. The chimney's are taller, the rain volume and speed is worse and the crickets are bigger.

But there are a few interior factors using this chimney location. If you are able to get the chimney located at a gable end or other tall spot within the house, more of the chimney is inside, correct? Thus, if you select a high-quality masonry finish to cover the chimney, more of it is on the inside. You get to see more of your investment and it has some thermal mass benefits. Another size-vs.-quality ratio comes into play. If the chimney works at an end gable, the total exterior area to cover is usually less since the gable wall portion is exposed inside. Thus, cultured, more expensive stone (stack style) can be used on the inside tall face, while the three exterior chimney sides can be covered with a veneered, natural, more rugged stone exterior. This cost ratio between the two stone technologies averages closer to the lower cost, yet still yields a quality result.

11

The Lawnmower Treadmill

I suspect that most people don't like mowing as much as the first-time homeowner, who gleefully explains that they "get their exercise" from this weekend task. Part of the downsizing effort should be making your outdoor landscape even less of a contributor to the treadmill burden. Also, the building-Green movement continues to point out that water costs will rise significantly. And, the chemical treatment of lawns has its own burden. Keep-it-simple techniques should be applied outside your last home also.

First, to add some credibility to my hunch about the lawn-mowing dislike, factor in two key elements. The people that are of concern here, the older baby-boomers, have been through a few, if not several, home changes. They also have the advantage, or pain, of time in their favor.

They have long passed the initial glee of one's own first home and the fun of fixing up the yard. The kids are long gone, and even the possible grandkids are using the backyard only on rare visits. The need for the football and volley ball games is also gone. Guess what is still lingering around? The grass — and that monster is winning!

Over time, this effect is in almost any neighborhood that has had some long-term baby-boomer owners or recent move ins preparing for a life transition. Since we can't possibly have an unlimited database of time-lapsed photography over this huge American suburbia, I'll use my database alone and bet it is a good microcosm of the United States. I have traveled for well over thirty years in principally four of metro-Atlanta's largest counties. Each county now has over 600,000 in population are loaded with a vast array of different suburban subdivisions. I have lived in three of them — each one for years. I now see more rural-county scenes. But as I have visited some familiar neighborhoods and homes over these long periods, I have noticed a slightly hidden symptom of grass dislike. In the south, with our natural abundance of pine trees, we have what I label the *creeping pine island*. That is, over time, the pine straw zones (pine trees circled with straw), typically with a tree or more in the yard (sometimes with other plant elements), grow annually. Grow they do — until the pine islands are king! I have seen many yards where the remaining grass is only one or two mower-widths wide. (I am not about to calculate the rate at which this happens.) It simply is OK to not want to mow your lawn anymore! The difficulty lies in neighborhood peer pressure and the momentum of change. But we are changing anyway — some of us are planning to move into a last home, even if we are nervous about this ominous name.

Keep it simple is relevant here. It does not mean that one gives up gardening if it is one of their hobbies, but to involve it in this new approach. For example, in my neighborhood, there is what I refer to as a good example of "house placement" — possibly by accident — maybe by planning, is occupied by a retired couple. It incorporates many of the concepts that we have discussed. It is on a sloped mountain lot, is a ranch house on a basement, has a garage on upper level with easy access to the house. The clincher is that their stone-covered garage wall is bermed into the hill cut before the main road. This area, from this wall to the main road, is their garden hobby zone. No lawn to mow, just a range of plants and landscaping techniques that are natural. I know their work is admired everyday by drivers passing by.

The available-water reality is hitting newer growth areas in the United States, such as our Southeastern states. One downside of this growth is demonstrated in the recent drought conditions there. In fact, Georgia, Alabama and Florida are feuding over water ratios of a principal river shared by the region. Specific local and state government edicts have banned any watering outdoors. One nearby county, without a major river within its boundaries, buys old marble quarries as a source for groundwater for their growing needs (fueled by nearby Atlanta's escape crowd). Western regions of the United States have dealt with this water-limit problem for decades. The new reality of the commercial building industry, as exemplified by the LEED points for landscaping, (not having grass lawns or turf and its associated water burdens), indicates that we need to do things differently.

All these water-cost symptoms and the time burden urges me to advocate what I have been doing in my own home for years and is extremely relevant now. Again, keep it simple, and plan the outside of your new home so that it is not a burden. Note how some of the drier Western regions utilize native species, like cactus, mixed with natural items, such as rocks, for the bulk of their exterior space. In our Georgia Appalachian mountain area, with rocks ranging from any old stone to the beautiful quartz, native materials are being utilized.

Now specific regional information sources and landscaping specialists can build on these basic tenets. An example, in this short section, involves this mix of natural elements and the low-maintenance concepts discussed about the house. Earlier, I talked about the need to balance the size, shape and orientation of the house into the natural slope of the region's terrain. I also stressed minimizing the impact to the natural environment, like not digging and cutting more than required to build the home (rectangle vs. square going down the hill). There are two cuts into the hill and the reality of making the transition from these zones requires design, physical work, material and hopefully not much of the dreaded maintenance. The choice of materials

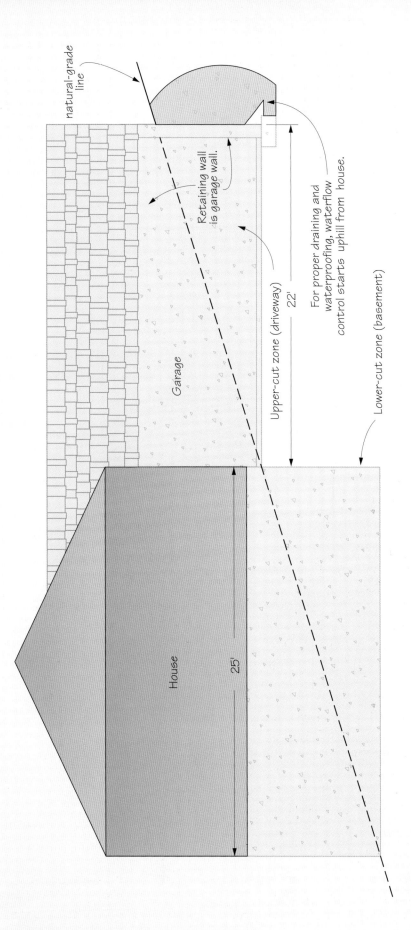

Figure 11.1 Garage placement on sloped lot.

Finished grade line

garage concrete retaining wall (uphill from house)

8'

concrete retaining wall

Finish rocks

4'

Garage depth a. r.

12'

example wall length

Figure 11.3   Driveway retaining wall taper.

Figure 11.2   Garage placement on sloped lot.

for the outside landscape have the same issues as the exterior of the house — don't select materials that will rot because they will need replacing. Cross ties and pressure treated wood walls do not have long-life spans.

An example is the landscaping issue (and the house placement on a tough, sloped lot) that was discussed by a realtor friend and I. He asked me to walk this property that he was representing and knew that the access to the house from the street was a negative for him selling it. He said that retirees were his likely clients. The extreme angle from the parking road to the actual front door was at best, a tough hike. With the grocery shuttle a typical task, a potential buyer would validate this as a deal-killer immediately. The realtor felt that the seller may be willing to invest in some way to improve this property's driveway access to aid in selling the property. As I walked the site and thought through options, I was beginning to get the hopeless feeling of the man falling 20 stories (14th floor, everything's OK). I knew that, with the house's position already committed, our options were severely limited. Note here that this is why the thinking-process investment, is so critical earlier than after you are falling. I was not able to come up with a good solution this late in the cycle.

But there is more. The client had already spent $10,000 for a pressure-treated, 4×4-fabricated retaining wall between the house and the road. I believe that even this amount (with more to come) would go a long way toward funding a better solution, if integrated with the foundation structure (poured, reinforced concrete) and with the house placement design. This wood wall, even with all the termite resistant chemicals, will fail. Ten years is a reasonable time to see this problem. And what is the replacement cost of the second wall? It will be more than the original amount. Also, it did not fully address the terrain-drop issue. If we had designed the landscaping/terrain needs at the time of the home design and placement, we would have invested in a more permanent concrete solution. We would have been able to soften the driveway

transition to the house at that time. Now, it was simply a mess. By the way, the owner did spend more money later for an additional, large concrete structure which provided a parking area for cars at the higher street level. Thus, a wooden set of stairs still had to assist the people to walk down to the front door. (And yes, gravity won on the return trip back up to the car!) Note that two other compounding factors also arose. It's easy to guess now that the wooded stairs will have maintenance issues. But what the exposed new concrete? Due to our community guidelines, this had to be covered. In this case with the expensive, but preferred stone. And yes, we still had a height issue with this parking zone. So, safety railings were needed at the top of this new walled area. The bottom line is that the major problem, after all this expense later than earlier, is still there!

A summary of this case is that not only the timing of the planning stage, but that the materials, preferably locally natural are best. Even with the best of design intentions and using solid techniques such as concrete retaining walls for the bulk of the structural terrain issues, minor surprises occurred.

> Keep it simple, and plan the outside of your new home so that it is not a burden.

The formed concrete retaining wall, even shaping to adapt to the natural terrain, will not be perfect. When the final grading and shaping are done, there is almost some transition, say a 2-3'-high concrete end wall. Figure 11.3 is an example of trying to continue the retaining wall to the actual terrain. The finished terrain needs to smoothly continue and taper off. I frequently see contractors build another small wooden wall (cross-ties or pressure treat) for this small transition zone from the concrete to the ground. Forget this band-aid, just use a large native boulder or two with smaller rocks smoothing out the transition, which will match the should-be, stone-faced concrete wall. Masonry-based blocks for short retaining wall sections are good alternatives. I have seen home-building sites where the beautiful native rock is hauled away (cost) during grading and months later a wood-versioned mini-zone is created (cost again). Then the wood structure is replaced years later.

Figure 11.4 Local, natural-rock retaining wall.

Using natural rock for terracing the bulk of the landscape, which is covered with either natural, no-water plants, mulch or wood chips from the original tree removals, are continuations of this concept. I trust that this simple start will send you on your own outside landscaping journey. Simply adapt, don't modify!

GARAGE LOCATION

To cross-relate some of the needs of our clients with the low-energy and low-maintenance issues and further linked to landscaping factors, the garage location on a sloping lot offers an opportunity for a solution.

Place the garage near the main house level and bermed into the upper cut of the terrain. Figure 11.1 shows the importance of using the upper hillside structural wall of the garage as the retaining wall of the garage (and very likely the garage backside wall). This wall can taper down, or as appropriate, adapt to the natural flow of the terrain out the driveway. An interesting appearance benefit of this application is that the garage and home now seem to "fit into" the terrain, rather than awkwardly protrude above it. The above-grade portion of the bermed garage wall, show in Figure 11.2, demonstrates this terrain meshing, while limiting the amount of exterior wall to be stone covered (more expensive = less/more). This wall transition zone, when coupled with proper water-proofing and drainpipe routing, provides an uphill beginning to water control long before the house. As this retaining wall drops to 18-24"-high, single large boulders, vs. the expensive poured concrete wall would be a natural and practical alternative (see Figure 11.3). If this is not done soil erosion will occur, even in this small area.

Figure 11.5 Walnut Ridge Energystar home.

Another important by-product of this garage location is an overall improvement in low-energy design and safety issues. This is because the garage door, always a leak point in the building envelope, is not near the living section of the house. By the way, while writing this section, friends had just returned from a holiday trip and found a broken water line from their hot water heater. Yes, it was near the garage and the garage was a drive-under in a typical two-story chalet. The cold weather, while gone, froze the line, bursting the pipe and causing water damage. The garage door sealing was within the main building envelope. Not the first time I have heard of this! With the garage location near the main level it is easier unloading groceries up there where kitchen is, rather than down here where basement is.

Figure 11.4 shows a section of retaining wall 2-3' high. Note that as the wall requirements are taller,

structural issues and safety take precedence. For walls about this height, with substantial base rocks, and some artistic effort, a natural-appearing wall can be built. We obtained these rocks nearby from a large shopping center project (unfortunately clearing a large and beautiful mountain area) with minor hauling charges. (Note the short distance for you guys keeping up with LEED mileage points!). An hour or two of bobcat time was the bulk of the effort invested for this wall section. Despite the need for a concrete drive on this steeper mountain location, we still had a small gravel drainage zone on both sides of the driveway for more natural water seepage and also soil erosion control as seen in the foreground of Figure 11.4. It's best to use a qualified landscaper for these projects if they are beyond your abilities. These examples are presented to set the tone of a positive landscaping approach that won't land you on a treadmill.

12

The Final Recipe

Now that we have this wide set of varying ingredients that may result in a good "Last Home". How could we mix them all up and derive something sane? A real project, The Walnut Mountain EnergyStar House, is an excellent example that will demonstrate these concepts at work. First, I will relate the history of the project from conception through the actual building steps, both with trials and triumphs. At the end, we will review the owner's feedback from living in the project. The owner's responses to the structured questionnaire form I prepared, plus their own candid comments will also be shared.

First, our building site is a North Georgia mountain gated complex (Walnut Mountain) near the town of Ellijay, located about eighty miles due north of Atlanta.

We are also only 30 miles south of the North Carolina/Tennessee juncture. We thus are close to a mid-range United States climate zone, with slightly more Southern (warmer) weather bias. As hinted at in earlier trending discussions, our Gilmer County growth mirrored many of these factors. Our current full-time population is about 25,000 with the 1980's level around 15,000. On peak weekends, like during popular October Apple Festival periods, weekend guests can swell the actual totals in the county toward 50,000 (by weekend-only homes). Note that the increase in ratio of the baby-boomer sect is more than represented with the expected retired segment added to the original true "natives". As referenced prior, our family added to this baby-boomer group by moving away from the hectic Atlanta scene much earlier than originally considered. In fact, our daughter was just in the midst of middle-school. (This was initially a small crisis of change!)

Now while developing my Residential Design business and evolving the Timber-Truss system, I noticed this divergence pattern between weekend-ers vs. retirement homes. I was quite firm on the main-floor living issue as demonstrated in our own designed cabin. I regularly advised clients to ensure that the master bedroom was on the main level even if the home was a two-story design. I began to finally see this master-on-main wording actually showing up in print on local realtor's advertising. After several of my own projects using the steeper 12/12 pitched Chalet-style Timber Trusses as well as projects designed for "spec" builders with conventional framing, I pushed forward with another generation of Timber Trusses. This version emphasized one key factor: Lower truss pitches with the mating floor plans targeted for single floors (ranches, or more specifically cathedral ranches). See Figure 7.7 (8/12-20 truss in shop) for reference. Another goal was achieved in that these trusses were "more rustic" because they had fewer steel plates due to design intent and the fact that they structurally supported the roof only (20 pounds minimum per square foot load rating) and not both the roof and the second floor (30 pounds plus the 20 pounds). Since the trusses now could be at 6' spacing, rather than 4', less trusses per house was enhanced (less/more). This spacing plus more wood exposed seemed to reach a balance of "rustic", but not too rustic and not too much mass.

With and during the evolution of this new ranch/rustic-style trusses, I developed floor plan ideas using these sized trusses as building-block modules. I want to reinforce the "with" idea above. The general sizes are derived from several intersecting issues, but mainly they enable good useful room sizes and good roof pitches. With sets of these type trusses I now have room module sizes that fit a good range of home sizes (maybe not McMansion size). Developing a series of floor plans over the years resulted in one that I called No.14C. You guessed it, 14A and 14B were smaller and so on. My standard 14C was about 1,650 sq. ft. in a 2-bedroom, 2 bath-configuration on the main floor over a matching basement footprint.

Figure 12.1 is the Walnut Mountain EnergyStar Model home floor plan that evolved from the basic version No.14C.

How this floor plan evolved into a real house is the next tale. Richard, my band-aid/broken-leg contractor friend was in transition with his own career in 2005. Despite a long history of his family in construction, Richard had just sold a related business and was now moving forward to be a full-time general contractor. His dad, R.C., also of a carpenter background, had recently moved to our community. Richard and R.C. were planning to team up in this construction endeavor. Richard and I had done Timber-Truss projects together for years on a project-by-project basis. In fact, Richard frequently helped out in my shop building the trusses and also at the actual site. He also had a desire to not just build the same old house that he saw in the local market. Richard had purchased an earlier set of my Timber Trusses, used in a display area, now occupied by this new Rustic-style display. His plan was to use this small truss kit for a future personal hunting-cabin core. As we discussed ways of using these 12/12-pitched Chalet trusses to build a cabin on another lot he owned in my own Walnut Mountain development, things took another path. Even though his lot was sloped, it was buildable. The floor plan ideas using this style didn't seem to fit the property unless he wanted a little weekend cabin, which he didn't. We were at a crossroads with his plans.

About this time, I was thinking that I needed to refine this family of floor plans more than the clients wanted. For example, one of my current

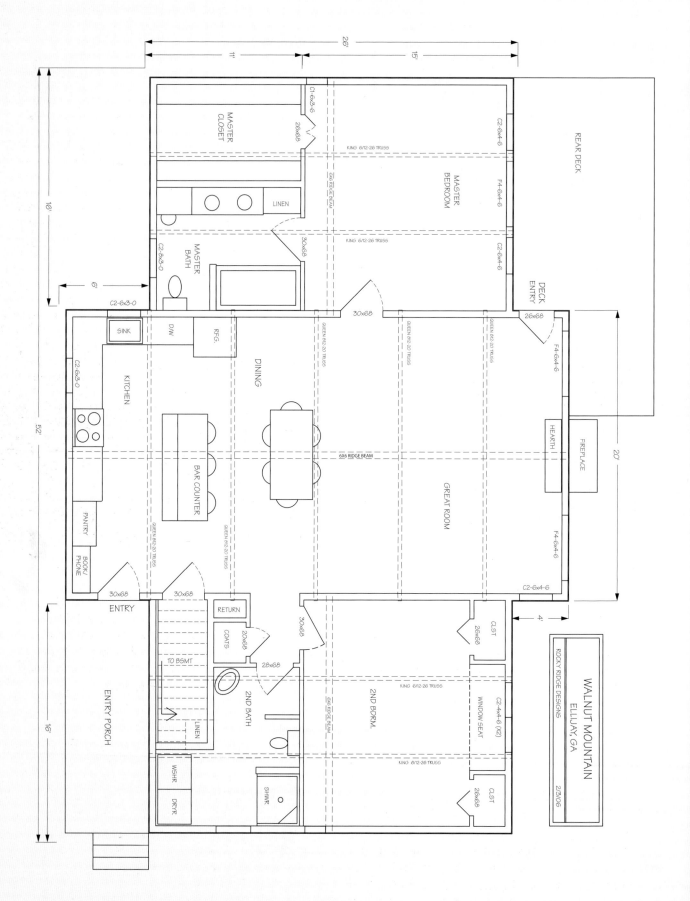

Figure 12.1 Walnut Mountain Energystar house floor plan.

Figure 12.2 EnergyStar house elevation view.

client's project, the Library House (Figure 10.1) was their own vision of their last home. It had the specific items that were special for them, including a beautiful library and over 2,000 sq. ft. (over basement) on the main floor. I wanted to focus more on the low-energy and low-maintenance factors in a 1,500-1,600 sq. ft. footprint. With my knowledge of the EnergyStar program, I felt utilizing a standard, a national recognized format (EPA) was a key beginning. Also, we could employ SouthFace, based in Atlanta, to test and certify the house to that standard. SouthFace is a nationally-respected, non-profit organization that promotes building-Green concepts. SouthFace had partnered with the Atlanta Home Builder's Association to develop a more complete residential-building guideline program called EarthCraft. Note that the national level LEED For HOMES new certification process from the USGBC

(United StatesGreen Building Council) is a superset of EarthCraft. Both programs utilize the EnergyStar guidelines as a core for the energy use. Therefore, my primary goal for one of my projects was to build to EnergyStar guidelines and have a floor plan that was in the mid-range of my typical client's needs. Thus, Richard, R.C. and I decided to take the risk and build this model home version. This action would test out our ideas that we thought focused on a retirement home, not just a weekend cabin. Thus, the idea of the Walnut Mountain EnergyStar Model Home was born!

Before I delve into the gory steps of us actually building this home, I will present an overview of the Walnut Model floor plan to highlight some of the concepts presented and employed in this model. Figure 12.1 shows the floor plan of the house shown in Figure 12.2. Note that the basic

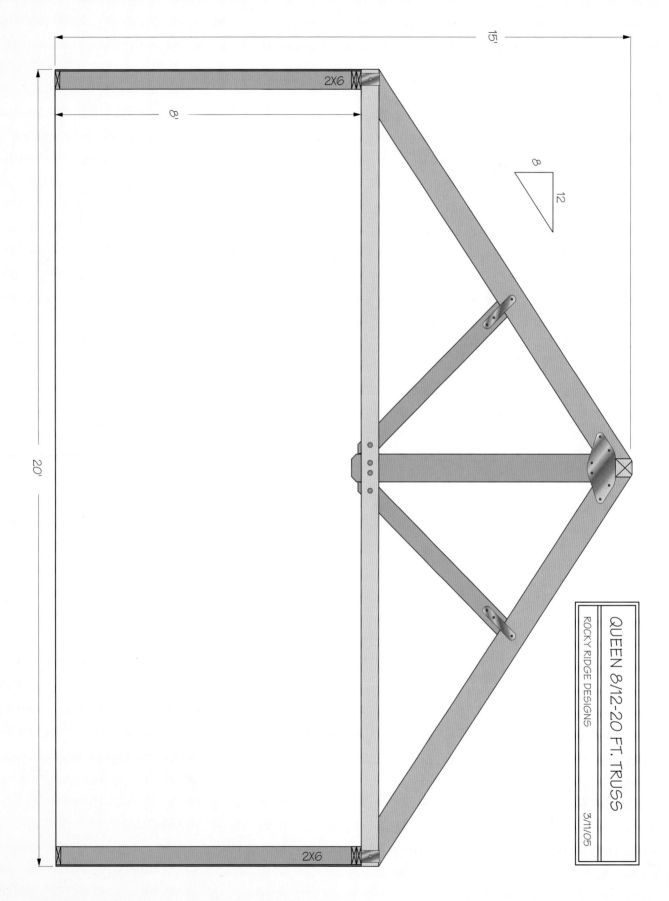

Figure 12.3 Timber truss – Queen 8/12-20ft.(great room).

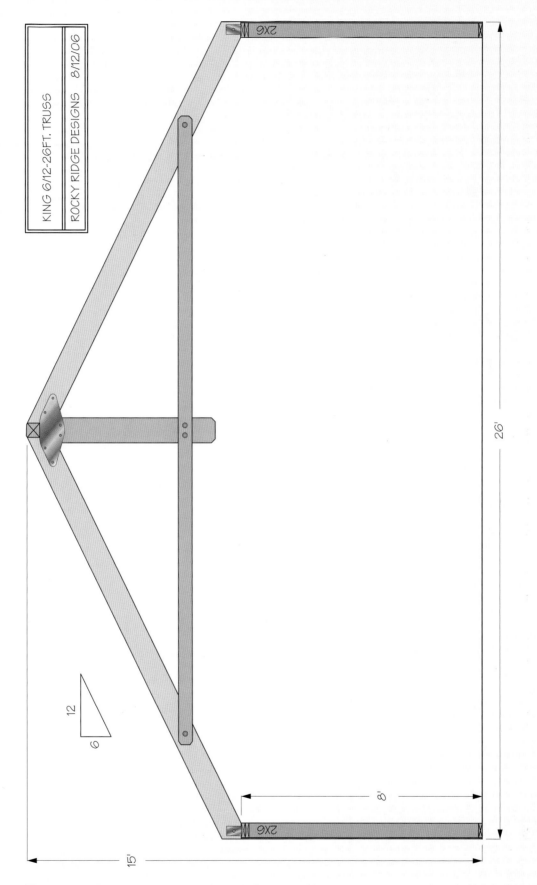

Figure 12.4 Timber truss – King 6/12-26ft.(bedrooms).

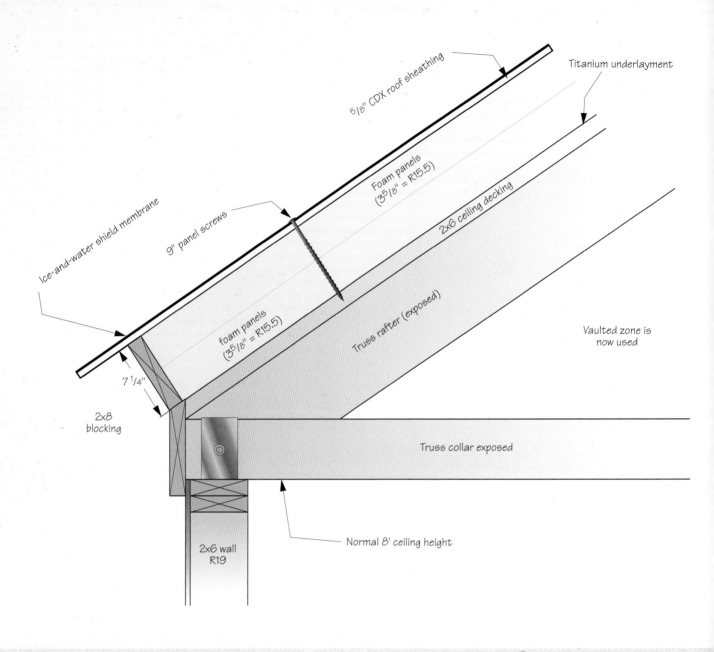

Figure 12.5   Timber truss roof details.

footprint is roughly a rectangle with a slightly more complex shape. This slight increase in complexity is the reality that most American clients do not want a plain house (our parents "ranch"). The central 20'×36' great room is a rectangle that is crossed by a longer rectangle that is 26'×52' (go horizontal). The roof crossing the two sections produces the valley in the middle of the roofs. The great room "open" module is formed with just five Queen 8/12-20' Timber Trusses as shown in Figures 7.8 and 12.3. The two wings flanking either side of this central public area are the bedrooms. These bedroom modules are formed by King 6/12-26' Timber Truss

pairs as shown in Figure 12.4. Both these trusses have about the same inner ceiling height — a cathedral ceiling, but at a reasonable 15'-high maximum at the ridge peak (go horizontal) and not the overpowering 22'-23' for a typical Mountain Chalet (roof-pitch penalty). Another way to think about this ceiling height is that the average of the peak height at the ridge and the normal 8'-high wall is 11½'. Why increase the normal wall height to 9' or 10' walls when you already have a cathedral ceiling? The entry side of the house — the high side of the hill slope — tends to have the more utility functions of the home, like closets and bathrooms. Thus

Figure 12.6 Energystar house great room and fireplace.

the primary spaces, with larger windows, are on the other side where the mountain view exists. Figure 12.2 shows the elevation where the view exists, not the road access (curb-appeal penalty) side. If we rotated the house to make this elevation fit the road, the view would be lost (unless you prefer to only look at the road). This house placement decision occurs more often than not. Look at the stair location for going down to the basement (no need for them to go up to the second floor, think horizontal). They are in the "back" of the house, against the concrete foundation wall bermed against the earth. Basically they are out-of-the way and not intruding into the prized basement daylight space on the view side. This layout is very space efficient with no wasted halls, walls, etc. (less/more) on a 1,550 sq. ft. footprint and yet has the warmer wood ceiling feeling (Casual-Timber style). We chose non-wood colors (personal taste choice, of course) in some areas to prevent the over-use of one beige

color. This design enables future color changes at a minor cost on a room-by-room basis.

Let's discuss a few technical details of our non-vented roof design. We believe that it is a good meshing of the three most important basics: Quality, low-energy use and casual-cabin feel. These details are shown in Figure 12.5. The 2×6 fir tongue-and-groove decking is nailed right on the *top* of the Timber Trusses. This provides the desired wood look inside (Casual Cabin) plus the incredible strength of this thicker material (less/more). On top of the decking we added a high-grade roof underlayment, such as Titanium. This is done for three reasons. First, we want to immediately protect, from weather, our clients investment during the first few days of construction. Second, it is imperative, in non-vented designs that it is really "non-vented". This means tight sealing, no places for moisture to move either in or out. And third, if a leak ever develops, we want to save the main

Figure 12.7 Energystar house kitchen.

structure of the house first, with insulation and trim the lower cost issues. On top of the underlayment is the 7¼"-thick EPS foam sheet insulation (R31 with borate treatment). We split this into two 3⅝"-thick halves and offset any joints between layers as an extra thermal break. We have the hot-wire, foam-cutting tool plus a custom table, with pre-set angles, to expedite the foam-fitting process.

With the foam installed, the ⅝"-thick CDX plywood (42% thicker than typical 7/16"-thick OSB decking on conventional vented roofs) is added. Around the outer perimeters, the 2×8 blocking pieces naturally fit the 7¼" space. We caulk the inside of this perimeter framing prior to the foam panel insulation. The CDX top sheathing is secured to the 2×6 tongue-and-groove decking with 9"-long SIP screws. (This pattern of self-drilling drilling screws

is a typical 3×3 array, or nine per 4×8 sheet of CDX. This panel-screw pattern nets a holding force of each sheet at over two tons, even with a conservative rating on these high-strength SIP screws.) Considering that homes of this size use from 55 to 65 plywood sheets, one can estimate the total high-wind resistance here. Each 2×6 roof decking board under is attached with two No.16 framing nails to each of the timber trusses. We caulk ⅛"-wide gaps between panels with a SIP supplier caulk/adhesive. Where a CDX sheet overlaps the border 2×8s, typical sheathing nailing occurs. Then, we cover the entire CDX top sheathing with a WR GRACE, Ice/Watershield, self-adhesive membrane. This key step provides double insurance against roof water leaking and moisture penetration into the roof insulation area. All of these process steps above the

Figure 12.8 Energystar house master bedroom window view.

timber trusses adds a net increase of several dollars per square foot over the typical roof. But increased roof structure strength, better insulation and attractive interior cosmetics are all achieved with this approach (less/more). With just the three workers doing all of these steps under our direct testing control and comparing to the labor times of other crews on other projects, we believe our estimates are good. The results should be obvious.

Now with the general house description outlined, let's look at a few details of the great room space. The goal in this public area is to have an open feel and be somewhat spacious, but within a realistic square footage budget. This 20'×36' area enables a kitchen, dining and living room to be connected, but stacked vertically. Our feedback experience shows that this 720 sq. ft. area meets this comfortable, yet roomy balance. Typically we see weekend cabins that have about 500-600 sq. ft., at best, for these three functions. We also placed the chimney at the gable end (simpler roof design) peak with the interior side being stacked cultured stone as shown in Figure 12.6. Despite the apparent penalty of the fireplace here on this prized view wall, the two large fixed picture windows are still accomplished. (All windows are low-maintenance, aluminum-clad, EnergyStar rated units.) The bump-out shape of this gable end enables a door on one side for deck entry and a venting egress casement window on either side. Thus, this slightly more complex shape provides more window/door places, somewhat offsetting the gable-end fireplace location penalty. We have also received feedback that some clients prefer their TV/Entertainment

Figure 12.9 Energystar house window seat.

the side of this area due to the tighter mountain lot dictating the entry porch here. A possible variation to this shed porch, side approach, is a gable-roof-style porch off the end of the kitchen gable, which is permitted on a larger building site.

This roof structure is the high-performing, non-vented roof system as shown in Figure 12.5. Even though we used a "hybrid" Timber Framing system we did not compromise the quality of the roof structure in the bedrooms just to make the great room pretty. Only in filling in the small valley section between the central module ridge to the two bedroom wings was conventional framing used. This area was sprayed with R30 foam insulation and made a non-vented space. This conventional framing section did not cut into nor alter the higher-quality concept, but simply filled in on top. We averaged this higher cost timber-like structure by having less roof pitch and then using the exposed "attic" area (which is usually sealed up as non-vented attic) as living (less/more). The *entire* main living floor, the primary living space for most people, is enveloped in this Timber Truss, warm wood environment (casual cabin).

The next primary space is the master bedroom. Its 16' long side (could be 18') is oriented to maximize window area along the view side. Figure 12.8 shows the three-window combination of center view (fixed) and two flanking venting (casement) windows on this wall. We also have a small casement window on the side wall which functions to provide cross-flow fresh air for the room and another daylight source from a different wall. (Comfort.) Even if this wall is East or West oriented, the heat gain is moderated by its size, a quality window choice (SHGC factor) and only exposed to the sun during part of the day. This small step pays dividends to the overall room environment.

The master closet and master bath are intentionally located in the non-view side of the master bedroom wing module as a reasonable trade-off. The internal total wall length needed to finish this is simple, yet the resulting cathedral ceiling, even in this area, is a strong asset. The good sized bathroom also has this higher ceiling effect, with part of the King-version truss beams here. (Less/more and timber style.) The bathtub shown is a 36"-wide by 72"-long whirlpool size. Some clients may even squeeze in a second shower stall with the

downstairs in a separate den or a new high-tech thinner TV in the stoned area above the fireplace. The fireplace is a high-quality Canadian unit meeting R2000 standards for efficiency and sealing. It has an air pipe to the outside for air directly to the combustion chamber (low-energy usage and comfort). The kitchen area is wrapped around the back gable entry side of the house, providing more wall areas for cabinets as shown in Figure 12.7. We were able to provide two windows to offset the tradeoff (less/more) of not being on the view side. The convenient central bar/counter provides more counter and cabinet space as well as seating right at the kitchen area. This seating is a breakfast-only spot but, also provides convenient overflow dining seating for larger family gatherings when needed (less/more). One fact about these open floor plans is that the kitchen tends to be a gathering place during this family time. This particular bar location solves the conflict of the non-kitchen workers being nearby but not in the way. The main entry door opens to

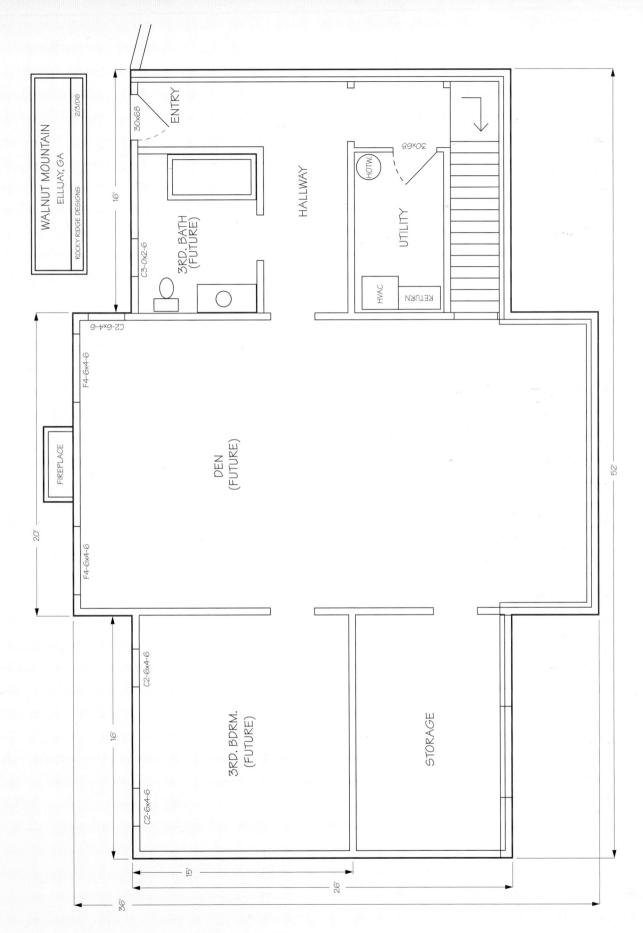

Figure 12.10 Energystar house basement floor plan.

Figure 12.11 Energystar house basement den wall.

appropriate compromises in the layout. The 18'-wide bedroom would be useful if this is a client's requirement. We have observed a surprising number of retiree clients requiring only a shower in the master bathroom, the opposite of having both. The result of this arrangement is that the master bath is private. In the respectable, downsized master closet this vaulted ceiling space will enable higher shelving if the owner desires to do seasonal clothes rotation and store the off–season articles higher up (less/more). I noticed that I rarely wear my sweaters from May to October down here in the south!

Let's go across the other side of the great room to the second bedroom. This wing is less important to most clients and some features are compromised for payoff in the master bedroom. The stairs from the main floor to the basement are located here with the resulting reduction in net space. To gain the closet space in the bedroom, we utilized the dual, small flanking closet, center-window-seat idea as shown in Figure 12.9. Even though this compromise was made in the prime view wall, the "specialness" of this resulting window nook is worth it. (Casual timber feel and less/more.) Using the higher-grade casement windows in the window nook over the seat means we can use a shorter window to meet the egress code issue. Two other benefits of using this more expensive window is that this moderate height provides storage under the seat and still have a safer wall barrier above the seat (a child would not be against a tall window). More of less/more. The net room size allows an optional bed with a small love-seat/bed combination while the bulk of the room could be a home office. The dual use of this room is in keeping with the majority of principal functions on the main floor. The ability to expand this wing module size while in the planning stage validates the modularity of this layout style. The extra two feet adds flexibility to this second bedroom as well as the back-half utility functions of this wing.

This second bathroom has less priority than the master bathroom. It is for the public (or for guests), so it's smaller. Note the very small hall area used to get to the public bathroom. Both a coat closet and the HVAC return are located here. This streamlined flow between zones translates into simpler internal walls, thus it has less framing and walls (less/more). Also, we were able to place a full-size washer and dryer in this second bath. I generally suggest clients consider having these two appliances installed in the back of the master closet if space and layout allows it.

Another goal is optimizing the basement for expansion of this ranch-style house. Figure 12.10 shows the layout of the EnergyStar basement. There are always trade-offs at each building lot. Our basement plan allow only one more bathroom and one more bedroom. The lot's terrain dictated the entry access to be in the upper right of the drawing. The resulting hallway through the daylight portion of this bedroom wing netted a nice future bathroom area. In a different building lot and with the 18'-wide bedrooms, this area could be a fourth bedroom or an office.

Moving toward the center of the basement, one of the gems of this layout emerges. The central 20'×36' zone under the main floor great room, enabled by the floor trusses, is a wonderful future open den space (less/more). Using only two-thirds to three-fourths of this space as a TV/media den is special. During the open house after completion (even during construction) we were rewarded with visitor's realization of this space's potential was atypical when compared to the small footprint of a normal mountain chalet

basement. Figure 12.11 shows the interior of the 20' view wall.

The third future bedroom is located in the upper left of the drawing. A more complete window arrangement can be implemented, based upon the owner's future plans. The rear section, or non-daylight portions of the basement floor plan have the utility functions. The primary needs, like bedrooms and dens generally use the higher-priority daylight areas where windows are located. This is a benefit of keeping the floor plan streamlined and diligently lining up both the main and basement functions (KISS). The resulting efficiency of the plumbing runs is evident, even with this particular lot forcing some compromise of the ideal.

The porch and the deck areas, very much slaved to the mountain lot terrain, are of moderate size but not tiny. Both units have low-maintenance EverGrain decking on the horizontal surfaces as well as the railing system. We believe substantial bracing on the taller, vertical deck posts as well as solid concrete footing are minimums.

The realities of building on a sloped lot will assist readers in their own planning. My project partner's lot was in the middle of the development, had a mid-level view and was about mid-sized (½ acre) with a nice mix of native hardwoods. A sprinkling of maple trees was a neat bonus and the benefits of their leaf color would be on display in the fall. With our ranch-like rectangle, the normal land apportioning practice of maximizing width to the street, the first test was the house placement. Mother Nature's natural terrain rarely allows us to have the slope exactly the way we desire. Despite a rectangular shape of 26' × 52', the need to rotate the house's position to fit this slope and the lot set-back rules required a sub-wall at the deep corner. We choose to optimize these factors vs. simply making the house "look good from the street". Another way to look at this process is we were acting as the client and working to achieve their goals rather than building another spec house just to make it easier to sell. We used 10"-thick poured, reinforced concrete walls.

> Mother Nature's natural terrain rarely allows us to have the slope exactly the way we desire.

The sub-wall sections, at 7' tall, then tapering off, had pilasters to increases strength and extra support for the basement slab floor. The fill-in for the sub-walls was packed and prepared. The slab floor had rebar in the deeper areas as well as 6×6 wire mesh in the slab. (I prefer wire mesh). Before backfilling, we used the Tuff-n-Dri foundation coating (flexible, not hard) and the matching Warm-n-Dri exterior insulation panels for an R10 value.

Exterior finishes, key to the low-maintenance goals, were carefully considered. We chose the Hardie, cement-based panel product for the bulk of the exterior. Since board-and-batten trim is accepted in our rustic community architectural guidelines, the Miratec composite trim met sustainability requirements. In the street-side gable end we applied a shingle section with some modest design elements, all done with the Hardie material and Miratec trim. We used one of the highest rated Sherwin-Williams paints to stretch the re-paint cycle to the maximum and still provide the owner with future cosmetic flexibility. Figure 12.2 shows the large exterior chimney area where we used the cost-effective natural veneer stone (stick-on) and the smaller interior area used the more expensive and attractive dry-stack cultured stone (a less/more tradeoff). Due to the lot terrain and the resulting sub-wall area on one house corner, more concrete had to be covered. We used complementing gray stucco. Even with the rectangle shaped ranch tradeoff vs. the square, two-story version, we would have had about the same concrete area to cover. The chimney height and area to be covered would have increased correspondingly with a taller format. That other choice would squeeze the cost-per-square-foot budget for a quality exterior material. The foundation rotation option, when one has the option to shift the house for the client's practical needs vs. just curb appeal, is demonstrated here.

With a general idea of what the EnergyStar Model Home could be, let's visit several key points along the building path. The three of us, Richard, R.C. and I, other than using major sub-contractors for grading, foundation, electrical and plumbing, were the principal work crew. Due to the importance of this project, I spent time away from my design and marketing efforts during this period. We wanted to test some building techniques and hybrid styles that would be difficult for the average small builder to do working out of his truck. For example, with my Timber Truss shop, and our 20' trailer capabilities, we could panelize more sub-systems than just the Timber Truss roof section.

This panelizing idea vs. hand-fabricating all the framing at the site had several positives as any larger, more progressive builder will understand. Besides the time spent at the site, with weather and waste hassles, we had other goals in mind. Beyond the SIP wall experience, we wanted to compare the labor-and-time and other cost trade-offs. For example, we noted in the SIP technical discussions that our nearest SIP module provider's standard width was 4', normally a good size to work with. However, with the cathedral ranch concept and setting the Timber Trusses at 6' centers, the cutting and piecing of the smaller SIPs lessened the building efficiency. The crossed module or bump-out shape of this floor plan set over a rectangle shape did not mesh well with the smaller SIPs. We felt that the 16' and 20' wall sections were good module sizes to work with. Since we planned to use a stronger, tighter sealing wall sheathing (Advantechs 5/8"-thick product), the transporting strength was better. Since a key goal was a tighter house, particularly since we planned for the EnergyStar door blower test, this tongue-and-groove and thicker sheathing would have less leak zones. We also wanted to compare the use of spray foam insulation and the inherent sealing characteristics. We planned to pre-build the six primary wall sections that represented 104 linear feet of the 176' home's main floor perimeter. These six wall panels fit on one trailer.

> With the unpredictable mountain winter-weather scheduling, the grading process always takes longer than desired.

With the unpredictable mountain winter-weather scheduling, the grading process always takes longer than desired. Our paneling approach actually complemented this frustration. Richard and R.C. were able to begin building these modules in my truss shop during the cold and wet weather days. Also, with saw beds and tables set up in the shop to handle the larger truss beams, productivity in cutting the framing material reached good levels for even this size project. Waste wood and sawdust was sent to fire our nearby wood-yard's drying kiln and not the local county landfill (could be LEED for Homes points!). As the weather interrupted our site working, more tasks were attempted in the shop to facilitate the later site work. Richard and R.C. completed all of the top- and bottom-plate layouts for the balance of the main floor and the basement portions. One key task completed was pre-cutting the stud sections, building all of the structural door and window headers and the wall junction T's. We utilized our SIP tooling and vender capabilities to pre-order the SIP foam in convenient sizes. These foam panel pieces were used in the header and T's to fully seal and insulate these modules. The R value of these modules went from a typical value of R3 up to R13 or R20. Both of these assemblies are significant leak zones in conventional stud framing. With the shop and atypical tools available to us, these sub-tasks were completed in advance and with less labor, including the loading and transporting to the site. When we began the framing process at the Walnut Mountain site, many sub-tasks were already completed.

The end gables above the main floor were shop-built. Since the end gables have to match the profile of the Timber Trusses, I provide a detailed drawing (using AutoCad) showing the exact stud lengths and angles for these gable modules. Since we had shop time available, I designed and fabricated steel "half" jigs of the two gable types (one to match the Queen 8/12-20' great room and the 6/12-26' King for the bedrooms). This investment in jigs may sound silly to the average contractor. I have stressed that some size standardization is needed in the building industry. Since we have shown that these few Truss sizes will fit a wide range of homes within our market segment, having many special sizes is not necessary. This is similar to one expecting that the typical 4×8 plywood sheet needs to be

offered in many sizes like 3.8' by 9.3' feet for each home built. (This alleged customizing is not so smart.) These few gable modules built in our shop with the jigs are far superior in quality and speed than the best craftsmen in the field can do. Those with manufacturing experience in other industries will understand this concept. Richard and R.C. efficiently built up these gables as half sections in advance. The shop productivity proved worthwhile in cutting all of these angles on a table setup rather than in the field with a hand-power saw.

Another level of productivity gain evolved with a mid-course correction. We had completed all potential work at the shop, but had rain at the building site, meaning no safe work could be done that day. In the shop, Richard and R.C. completed the half gables on our trailer, with the matching ridge post (to mate with the 6×6 ridge beam from the Timber Trusses). They completely sheathed each of the four main gables and applied the Tyvek exterior barrier, on the trailer. One quick delivery trip to the site and then unloading had these gable modules poised for installations for the later boom truck operation. With proper bracing, these ends could be lifted by the boom and installed the same day the Timber Trusses were being lifted. Another level of modularity rewarded us with completing another task early.

Before moving into the full building-site sequence, I want to say that the panel-module approach, with standard stud framing used here, also lends itself to more efficiency with larger SIPs. For example, we are evaluating another SIP supplier, with more shipping-distance factors, who has much larger wall capabilities and even higher insulating densities (more R-value or thinner wall/roof sections as desired). The six pre-framed wall panels noted earlier would now be six, 8'-high by 16' or 20' SIPs. The two, 26' gable main-floor ends could be subdivided into two smaller modules. The four bump-out sections can be implemented this way. With an additional eight, smaller SIP modules, the entire 176 linear feet of exterior main wall would be ready to go. With SIPs the wall insulation is included, as well as electrical chases and boxes. The level of productivity and quality can be increased, netting our customers a better end product.

Figure 12.12 Energystar house foundation walls.

BUILDING THE ENERGYSTAR HOUSE

I will now outline some of the major milestones of the construction sequence of the EnergyStar model. This project was completed with the labor of just three people, or, as Richard recounts "Me and two old men built it !" The poured foundation walls are shown in Figure 12.12 prior to filling in the sub-wall zones. The effect of the lot slope and the required house rotating to fit the lot are manifested in the sub-wall that was needed. Figure 12.13 shows the slab is being poured for the basement. Note the wire-mesh and re-bar steel reinforcement in wall load zones. In Figure 12.14 the foundation exterior waterproofing (Tuf/Dry) and R10 insulation (Warm/Dry) are being installed. While this out-side work was proceeding, Richard and R.C. were building the pre-framed main-wall sections in the shop as shown in Figure 12.15. Finally, basement framing starts in Figure 12.16. Note the pre-built headers and T's staged near the table saw. In Figure 12.17 the basement framing is completed. 12.18 shows all the main floor trusses installed. Notice the different pattern of the center 20' trusses with the two, outer-bedrooms corresponding 26' floor trusses. The basement floor under the 20' trusses requires no framing walls, thus this area is all open for future finishing (less/more). With the floor decking (3/4"-thick Advantech sheets) installed in figure 12.19, the main floor is ready for the walls.

Figure 12.13   The basement slab.

Figure 12.14   Energystar house warm-and-dry installation.

Figure 12.15   Pre-built walls sections in shop.

This project was completed with the labor of just three people, or, as Richard recounts "Me and two old men built it !"

Figure 12.16   Starting the framing on the Energystar house.

Figure 12.17 Basement framing is finished.

Figure 12.18 The floor trusses are installed.

Figure 12.19   Floor decking (covered).

Figure 12.20   The pre-made wall module raising sequence is starting with wall jacks As shown here, the wall module already have their protective exterior moisture barrier (Tyvek) attached.

Figure 12.21 Moving on, we can see the walls are erecting quickly. With only two workers, four walls are now in place.

Figure 12.22 Most of the exterior walls are now erected.

Figure 12.23 The few interior walls (for the great room with Timber Truss support) are filling in the main floor structure.

Figure 12.24 And finally, all the major walls, without the top gable sections, are erected and waiting for the boom truck and the Timber Trusses.

Figure 12.25   Before the boom truck is scheduled we need to assemble the Timber Trusses at the site (all pre-cut and ready to assemble). Figure 12.25 depicts this process with some of the units completed.

Figure 12.26   One of the King 6/12-26 foot bedroom wing Timber Trusses on the floor ready to be lifted by the boom truck.

Figure 12.27   One of the matching Gable-end walls is being lifted in place.

Figure 12.28 Near the end of the boom-truck-lifting day, most of the Timber Trusses are in place. Several hours of boom truck time, even on this tight mountain site, facilitated the erecting of the nine Timber Trusses and the four main Gable modules.

Figure 12.29 With the main structure sheaved and covered, a section of the built-up non-vented roof structure is shown. Note that the 2×6 pine tongue-and-groove decking, already nailed on top of the Timber Trusses, is covered by the Titanium roof covering layer (gray). Just to the left of this second bedroom wing roof, the very top membrane ice/watershield is visible (black) on the center great room section.

Figure 12.30 It's good insurance to cover the entire roof with the ICE/Watershield membrane as shown here. This completeness, beyond valleys or the typical northern application of Ice-damming prevention at the eaves, is important to long-term water resistance of the main structure. We have experimented with both horizontal and vertical applications since the adhesive qualities of the product are superb. The horizontal approach is the conservative technique.

Figure 12.31 The ice/watershield membrane sealing strips are visible around the window perimeter as well as entire building envelope's wrapping (TYVEK).

Figure 12.32 The tight-sealing interior shows a different technique. This is the rim area of the floor trusses in the basement. The high density foam is shown sealing places left marginally complete in typical construction with the usual result: air infiltration. This high-density foam is harder to control in consistency of application. However, the R value is so high (R7 per inch typical) that the average result is still very good.

Figure 12.33 The large, exterior Hardie cement panels are installed on the main-floor walls with some of the Miratec composite board/batten trim attached in the lower basement daylight level. Refer to Figure 12.2 to see the main elevation of the view side of the completed house.

CERTIFICATION PROCESS

With the house near completion, we scheduled Atlanta-based SouthFace to complete the EnergyStar certification process. Besides confirming the technical issues of the materials and processes used matched the design documentation, the actual blower door test was conducted. Specific confirmation on window labels meeting the EnergyStar levels for our climate zone is also a key step. The inspection and testing of the HVAC system is paramount. The location of the HVAC ducting within the building envelope is a fundamental design requirement. (In our cathedral-ranch approach, the bulk of the HVAC ducting is within the floor trusses in the basement.) The blower door test set up process was encouraging because the technician was sensing a well-sealed structure while calibrating his equipment. The blower test is conducted by attaching the blower assembly over an exterior door. With the fan in this assembly applying pressure to the entire house, and calibrating the pressure drop sensor to the house specifics, a leakage rate could be accurately measured.

This ACH figure, Air exChange per Hour, is essential in demonstrating how much of the entire volume of air within the house leaks out per hour (Leaks, not breathes!). The minimum value needed for EnergyStar is .35 ACH. A quick approximation of this figure is that a good house will leak about one-third of its air volume in one hour. The less the number the better it is. The Walnut Model tested at .05 ACH. We were very much in the range, or even better than a SIP-built house! This is real certified testing, not guessing.

Think over the above process for residential construction as compared to the electronic, the automotive and even the aircraft industries. Guess why these industries continue to improve their end product? The crucial step is that they *test* them prior to selling them to the client. Do we normally test our homes upon completion and prior to our client's purchasing the most important purchase of their life ? Ponder awhile on this one!

Two other HVAC issues related to both EnergyStar and owner comfort justify more discussion. First, EnergyStar requires balancing out this tight-house requirement with the fact some fresh-air intake, under control, is needed.

In Chapter 6 we discussed the two basic fresh-air intake approaches. On this modest-sized Walnut EnergyStar Model Home, a simple 4"-diameter duct from the HVAC air handler to the exterior, under electrical damper control, is utilized. This damper opens up when the HVAC blower (air handler) is cycling the condition air and closes when off. This small amount of fresh air during this operation assists in another energy-related matter. It equalizes the house's pressure when the HVAC is operating uncontrolled leak zones don't pull in outside air in the wrong place. (These "leaks" are the same "breathing" places in the house structure.) With our model home size and a very energy-efficient envelope, the small energy loss balances out with the fresh air needs of the owner (and comfort). As noted earlier, on a larger home than this model, an ERV (Energy Recovery Ventilator) or a HRV (Heat Recovery Ventilator) is recommended to regain this small amount of energy loss for this fresh air input. The ERV or HRV decision, aided by a quality HVAC sub-contractor, is determined by the heating or the cooling loads of the home being primary (Example: ERV's in South, HRV's in Northern climates).

The second HVAC-related enhancement is something we felt that is almost always lacking in the average home, but is acutely missing in the higher-pitched cathedral, or vaulted-ceiling homes. As noted in basic thermodynamics, we all know that heat rises, yet typical built homes seem to ignore this basic fact. Thus, we added a dual-return vent system to the EnergyStar model. Since we were using an 8/12-pitched great-room cathedral ceiling (on the high end of what we feel is practical), assisting the HVAC efficiency should be considered. Since we are in a more southern climate, cooling is a sizable energy load. The dual-return vent concept enables

> As noted in basic thermodynamics, we all know that heat rises, yet typical built homes seem to ignore this basic fact.

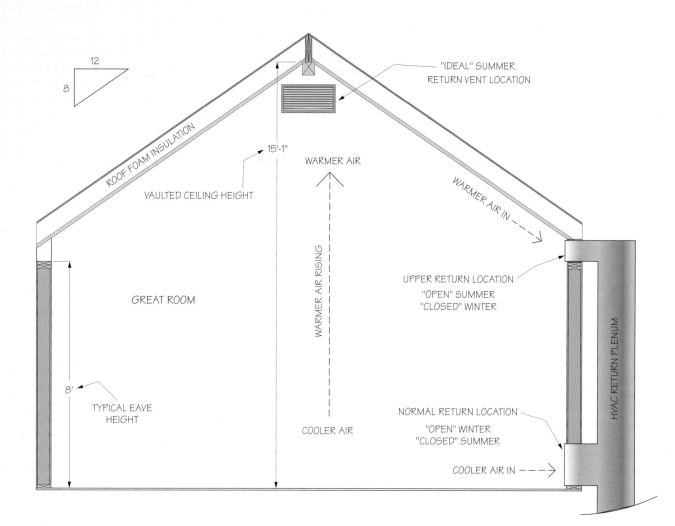

Figure 12.34 Dual-return vent concept.

the homeowner to use a lower return vent during the warmer months and a higher (nearer the roof peak than the floor) during the cooling months. Figure 12.34 shows this concept as utilized in the EnergyStar Model Home.

Since the HVAC return air is being sucked in closer to the opposite condition, the overall conditioning effect in the room is improved. Specifically, the HVAC is taking in air higher up in the room, thus intake air is warmer than the typical near-floor location during the cooling season (where the already conditioned, cooler air is concentrated anyway). The client closes one set of vents and opens the other set each half-year. Figure 12.35 shows the *upper* return summer vents. The winter unit is below, in the hall wall, closer to the floor as shown in Figure 12.36. This represents the location

we normally see. Note that both pictures indicate a vital clue not seen in the typical return grill: They both have adjustable damper levers typical for supply grilles but not for return grills.

For this Walnut project, we made a conscious compromise over the ideal drawing just shown. We choose the mid-level solution with the higher vent just above the typical eave height of 8'. Thus our summer return is more than two-thirds of the way (volume-wise) to the warmest ridge peak. Depending on the client's cosmetic tastes (wooden grilles?), the desired amount of maximizing the hotter air intake, and the physical layout of the ducting access, different levels of efficiency can be achieved. I suspect that the very high, ceiling-mounted, higher efficiency version may be too much of a cosmetic compromise for most

Figure 12.35 Upper return vents.

Figure 12.36 Typical lower return vent.

homeowners. Also, other floor plan layouts would facilitate maximizing this concept in a higher inner vertical gable wall much easier than disrupting the exterior sloped roof section that the Walnut house would have required. This improvement of several feet over the height difference in the single lower return vent locations is a solid alternative. This few-hundred-dollar option, even in our very-well-insulated structure, we feel enhances the client's comfort and is worth the investment. Ironically, the more decorative and even higher pitched, poorer insulated, taller homes we typically see in the market need this feature even more. Again, our default mode is to provide the client with more "comfort" for his investment value.

With the description of the EnergyStar Model Home construction process complete, we will transition to an unusual summary. The new owners will tell us of their experience of actually living in this unique model home.

13

Afterword

Naysayers.

There are and will always be.

But, keep doing the same thing over and over and see if anything changes.

A brief update on the Walnut Mountain EnergyStar Model home is appropriate here. The two new owners, Susan and Anita, decided to have Richard's remodeling crew finish out most of the  basement before moving in. Figure 13.1 shows the final basement floor plan that fit their needs. Thus, the finished floor space, by combining the main floor with the portion finished in the basement, came to almost 2,800 sq. ft. One rough number comparison of before and after should assist the reader in the real applications of the strategies presented. The EnergyStar house selling price, if counting only the main floor, prior to finishing the basement, came to about

$173 per square foot for finished space in mid-2007. This figure includes everything: land, labor, sub-contractor fees, contractor fees, Timber Trusses, real-wood ceilings, realtor commission, bank interest and so on. At about the same period in our community, resales and new homes of average construction ran from $140-$160/sq. ft. For about 15% more, high quality is achieved. But wait, when the basement was finished and the two owners moved in, the actual cost came in at about $106/sq. ft. for the total heated and cooled living space. On the energy front, the owner's first two months of utilities (total electric) average was about $100 per month.

For a good reference, I prepared a simple one-page questionnaire for the new owners, Susan and Anita, to complete. They graciously supplied their feedback. Note that on the form is a large comment section for their specific thoughts as well as the structured necessary information. Figures 13.2 and 13.3 are reprinted as submitted by them.

We trust that their feedback is some validation that there truly is a need for a *last-home* market for the momentum of the American baby-boomer's retirement. Sounds simple, but less-is-more is at work again, but inversed. People usually build such a big house, in the beginning, that they don't completely utilize the poorly-built basement space. If they do finish out the basement in an already substantial home, netting a huge house, then they are only again feeding the treadmill.

An intersecting of two sub-trends can be overlooked by those naysayers, but could be melded into our baby-boomer retirement dilemma's solution. That is, the shift of baby-boomers downsizing and moving out of suburbia is real and substantial. Pick any number from 20 to 40% out of a total of 76 million baby-boomers that are predicted to downsize. Spread it out over ten years or so, it's a huge number. This is still at least 300,000 new homes per year out of 1 million-plus built annually. This will not stop within a generation; it is a MegaTrend. This is one of the largest impacts to the United States economy ever.

> The shift of baby-boomers downsizing and moving out of suburbia is real and substantial.

What are boomers leaving behind? A lot of big, empty houses, mainly in suburbia, with some closer to urban centers. The second half of this equation is that the baby-boomer's children have a need for these larger homes during their child-rearing years. To close out this second half of the solution, these larger, almost-new to mid-age structures, need improvement with the same low-energy, low-maintenance factors. Rather than continue building a wave of brand new McManisons or dream houses with all of the related sprawl problems, we need to focus on upgrading (insulation, windows, hi-efficiency HVAC, etc.) the existing homes being vacated. I believe there will be a glut of these vacated, larger, high-cost homes on the market. Just more residue from the baby-boomer's wake.

Rather than focusing on new construction for a market that will have excess inventory anyway, let's focus on the new market that will have long-term positives for America, the baby-boomer's *last* home.

We can and must change. I hope the baby-boomers step up to accept our generational challenge. Our parents were the greatest generation. We don't have a dictator to rally us as in World War II, but we do have a great enemy. It is us and our current chosen lifestyle. Paraphrasing Winston Churchill, from the greatest generation's burden, "We must do what is needed."

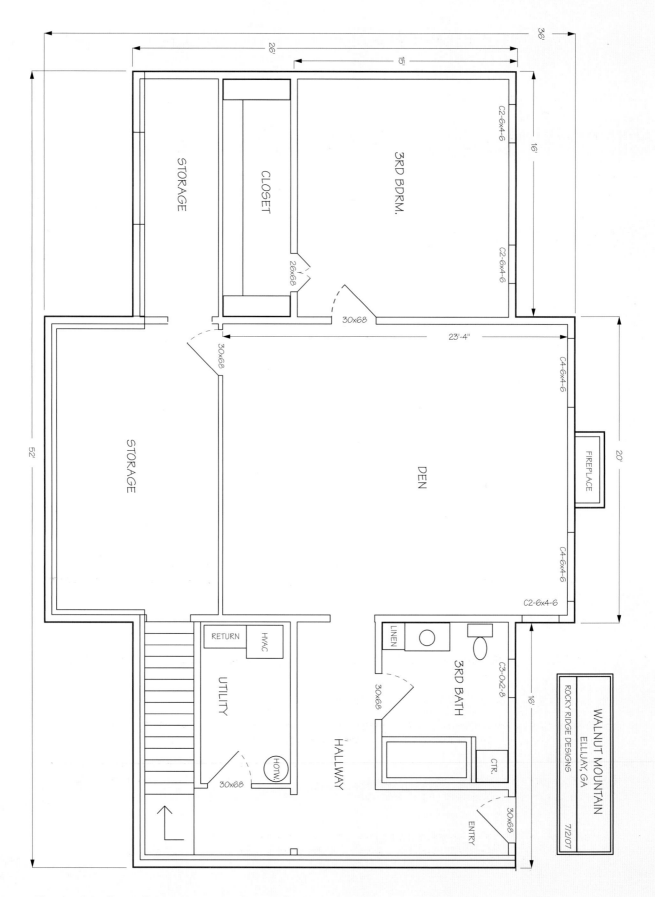

Figure 13.1 Owner finished basement floor plan.

ENERGYSTAR MODEL HOME EVALUATION

CLIENT: SUSAN   DATE: 2/21/08

DETAILED FEEDBACK

ROOM	THERMAL COMFORT	PHYSICAL COMFORT	SIZE	LAYOUT	NATURAL LIGHTING	FAVORITE	SUBTOTAL
GREAT ROOM	10	10	10	10	10	10	60
KITCHEN	10	10	10	10	10	10	60
DINING	10	10	8	10	9	9	54
MSTR. BEDRM	10	10	10	10	10	10	60
MSTR. BATH	10	10	9	10	9	8	54
MSTR. CLOSET	10	10	9	9	N/A	9	
2ND BEDROOM	10	10	10	10	10	8	58
2ND BATH	10	9	8	10	9	N/A	
2ND CLOSET	N/A	N/A	7	9	N/A	N/A	
3RD BEDROOM	N/A	N/A	N/A	N/A	N/A	N/A	
3RD BATH	N/A	N/A	N/A	N/A	N/A	N/A	
3RD CLOSET	N/A	N/A	N/A	N/A	N/A	N/A	
DEN	9	10	10	10	10	10	59
FRONT PORCH	N/A	N/A	9	10	N/A		
REAR DECK	N/A	10	10	10	N/A		
WINDOWS							
(IN GENERAL)	10	10	10	10	10	10	60

NOTE: RATE 1-10, 10 IS BEST

ENERGY COST SUMMARY TO DATE

MONTH	AUG 2007	SEP 2007	OCT 2007	NOV 2007	DEC 2007	JAN 2008	FEB 2008	AVG./MO.
COST	$48.21	$113.05	$103.12	$103.22	$127.64	$142.22		$113.30

Notes: 1 - During August 2007 approximately ½ of the month was doubled for averaging purposes.

   2 - Electricity (total) via rural EMC is approximately $.10 per kwhr (kilowatt per hour). Average usage per month approximately 1100 kwhr.

OWNERS COMMENTS

1 – LIKE MOST ABOUT HOME: The location and view of the mountains. Love the openness of the rooms and all the windows and the blend of cabin/home.

2 – LIKE LEAST ABOUT HOME: Would like to have separate laundry/mud room.

3 – CHANGES THAT YOU WOULD MAKE: Separate laundry/mud room. Doorbell and garbage disposal. The HVAC in the lower level could be better sometimes — the upstairs is comfortable while the downstairs is cool.

4 – MISC. COMMENTS: It's been my long time dream to live in the mountains and I feel very fortunate to have found this house that is both beautiful, livable and virtually maintenance free. The EnergyStar that was awarded to this house makes it cost efficient, which will allow us many years of contentment and peace.

Author's note:
HVAC supply vents need to be adjusted seasonally (main vs. basement). This will be monitored.
Basement door removed which makes the area fully open and impacts air balance (go horizontal, not vertical).

ENERGYSTAR MODEL HOME EVALUATION

CLIENT: ANITA   DATE: 2/21/08

DETAILED FEEDBACK

ROOM	THERMAL COMFORT	PHYSICAL COMFORT	SIZE	LAYOUT	NATURAL LIGHTING	FAVORITE	SUBTOTAL
GREAT ROOM	10	10	10	10	10	10	60
KITCHEN	10	10	10	9	10	10	59
DINING	10	10	9	10	10	8	57
MSTR. BEDRM	N/A	N/A	N/A	N/A	N/A	N/A	N/A
MSTR. BATH	N/A	N/A	N/A	N/A	N/A	N/A	N/A
MSTR. CLOSET	N/A	N/A	N/A	N/A	N/A	N/A	N/A
2ND BEDROOM	10	10	10	10	9	8	57
2ND BATH	10	9	10	10	10	7	56
2ND CLOSET	N/A	N/A	8	9	N/A	N/A	
3RD BEDROOM	8 **	10	10	10	8	9	55 **
3RD BATH	8 **	10	10	8	9	7 *	52
3RD CLOSET	N/A	9	9	8	N/A	8	
DEN	8**	10	10	10	10	9	57
FRONT PORCH	N/A	N/A	10	10	N/A	8	
REAR DECK	N/A	8	7	8	N/A	7	
WINDOWS							
(IN GENERAL)	10	N/A	10	10	10	10	

NOTE: RATE 1-10, 10 IS BEST

ENERGY COST SUMMARY TO DATE

MONTH	AUG 2007	SEP 2007	OCT 2007	NOV 2007	DEC 2007	JAN 2008	FEB 2008	AVG./MO.
COST	$48.21	$113.05	$103.12	$103.22	$127.64	$142.22		$113.30

Notes: 1 - During August 2007 approximately ½ of the month was doubled for averaging purposes.

   2 - Electricity (total) via rural EMC is approximately $.10 per kwhr (kilowatt per hour). Average usage per month approximately 1100 kwhr.

OWNERS COMMENTS

1 – LIKE MOST ABOUT HOME: The "outside" feel because of great windows, beautiful floors, beams and cabinets upstairs. Spacious feel throughout house.

2 – LIKE LEAST ABOUT HOME: Rear deck because of size and configuration.

3 – CHANGES THAT YOU WOULD MAKE: Move HVAC register away from countertop area, make rear deck larger and wraparound 2 sides, separate utility room and location of third bathroom.*

4 – MISC. COMMENTS: Overall, this house is very livable and aesthetically good. With large windows it "brings the outside" in and gives us a real feel for the mountains.

Author's notes:

* location: Due to septic limits, 3rd bath located in potential 4th bed zone (not allowed), opposite 3rd bedroom "wing"

** Anita uses 3rd bedroom in basement, adding middle picture window like in master = improvement and 2nd bedroom on main floor is reserved for guests

** HVAC supply vents need to be adjusted seasonally (main vs. basement). This will be monitored.

   Basement door removed which makes the area fully open and impacts air balance (go horizontal, not vertical).

References

AMERICAN ALDES VENTILATION CORPORATION
4537 Northgate Court
Sarasota, FL 34234
941-351-3441
www.americanaldes.com

CONSERV
727-375-8484
www.conserv.com

ENERGYEDGE, LLC
7701 E. Kellogg
Suite 722
Wichita, Kansas 67207
316-618-1983
www.energyedgeform.com

FEDERAL ALLIANCE FOR SAFE HOMES, INC.
flash.org

GRACE CONSTRUCTION PRODUCTS
na.graceconstruction.com

HUBER ENGINEERED WOODS
One Resource Square
10925 David Taylor Drive, Suite 300
Charlotte, NC 28262
800-933-9220

INFILTEC CORPORATION
800-349-7236
www.infiltec.com

RETROTEC ENERGY INNOVATIONS LTD.
1540 West 2nd Avenue
Unit #611
Vancouver, BC V6J 1H2 Canada
www.retrotec.com

RHEEM MANUFACTURING COMPANY
1100 Abernathy Road
Suite 1400
Atlanta, GA 30328
www.rheem.com

R-CONTROL STRUCTURAL INSULATED PANELS
AFM Corporation
211 S. River Ridge Circle #102
Burnsville, MN 55337
www.r-control.com

SOUTHFACE
www.southface.com

U.S. GREEN BUILDING COUNCIL
www.usgbc.com

TRANE
www.trane.com

UNITED STATES DEPARTMENT OF ENERGY
www.energycodes.gov/rescheck
www.epa.gov

BOOKS:
The Passive Solar Energy Book, by Edward Mazria, 1980 by Rodale Press

Building with Structal Insulated Panels (SIPs), by Michael Morley, 2000 by Taunton Press

Megatrends, John Maisbitt, 1982 by Warner Books

The Fountainhead, Ayn Rand, 1943 by Bobbs Merrill

www.choosinggreen.com   (Building Green information WEB Page)

www.energystar.gov   (EPA- EnergyStar Guidelines)

www.eco-structure.com   (Eco-Structure magazine)

www.edillon.com   (E. Dillon Company, Stone-looking brick)

www.fastenmaster.com   (FastenMaster – SIP Panel Screws)

www.finehomebuilding.com   (Fine Homebuilding magazine)

www.icc-rsf.com   (RSF Woodburning Fireplaces)

www.jameshardie.com   (James Hardie, cement exterior sidings)

www.miratectrim.com   (Miratec, composite trim

www.monierlifetile.com   (Monier, Concrete roof tiles)

www.nhab.com   (National Association of Homebuilders)

www.rockyridgedesigns.com   (Rocky Ridge Designs, "TIMBER" Trusses)

www.sips.org   (Structural Insulated Panel Association)

www.susanka.com   (Sarah Susanka – "Not So Big" Architects)

www.tuff-n-dri.com   (Trimco, foundation waterproofing & Insulation)

Suppliers

**ADAMS & KENNEDY —
THE WOOD SOURCE**
6178 Mitch Owen Rd.
P.O. Box 700
Manotick, ON
Canada K4M 1A6
613-822-6800
www.wood-source.com
Wood supply

B&Q
Portswood House
1 Hampshire Corporate Park
Chandlers Ford
Eastleigh
Hampshire, England SO53 3YX
0845 609 6688
www.diy.com
*Woodworking tools, supplies
and hardware*

BUSY BEE TOOLS
130 Great Gulf Dr.
Concord, ON
Canada L4K 5W1
1-800-461-2879
www.busybeetools.com
Woodworking tools and supplies

**CONSTANTINE'S WOOD
CENTER OF FLORIDA**
1040 E. Oakland Park Blvd.
Fort Lauderdale, FL 33334
800-443-9667
www.constantines.com
Tools, woods, veneers, hardware

FRANK PAXTON LUMBER COMPANY
5701 W. 66th St.
Chicago, IL 60638
800-323-2203
www.paxtonwood.com
Wood, hardware, tools, books

THE HOME DEPOT
2455 Paces Ferry Rd. NW
Atlanta, GA 30339
800-430-3376 (U.S.)
800-628-0525 (Canada)
www.homedepot.com
*Woodworking tools, supplies
and hardware*

LEE VALLEY TOOLS LTD.
P.O. Box 1780
Ogdensburg, NY 13669-6780
800-871-8158 (U.S.)
800-267-8767 (Canada)
www.leevalley.com
Woodworking tools and hardware

LOWE'S COMPANIES, INC.
P.O. Box 1111
North Wilkesboro, NC 28656
800-445-6937
www.lowes.com
*Woodworking tools, supplies
and hardware*

**ROCKLER WOODWORKING
AND HARDWARE**
4365 Willow Dr.
Medina, MN 55340
800-279-4441
www.rockler.com
*Woodworking tools, hardware
and books*

TOOL TREND LTD.
140 Snow Blvd. Unit 1
Concord, ON
Canada L4K 4C1
416-663-8665
Woodworking tools and hardware

**TREND MACHINERY &
CUTTING TOOLS LTD.**
Odhams Trading Estate
St. Albans Rd.
Watford
Hertfordshire, U.K.
WD24 7TR
01923 224657
www.trendmachinery.co.uk
Woodworking tools and hardware

WATERLOX COATINGS
908 Meech Ave.
Cleveland, OH 44105
800-321-0377
www.waterlox.com
Finishing supplies

WOODCRAFT SUPPLY LLC
1177 Rosemar Rd.
P.O. Box 1686
Parkersburg, WV 26102
800-535-4482
www.woodcraft.com
Woodworking hardware

WOODWORKER'S HARDWARE
P.O. Box 180
Sauk Rapids, MN 56379-0180
800-383-0130
www.wwhardware.com
Woodworking hardware

WOODWORKER'S SUPPLY
1108 N. Glenn Rd.
Casper, WY 82601
800-645-9292
http://woodworker.com
*Woodworking tools and
accessories, finishing supplies,
books and plans*

Index

More great titles from Popular Woodworking and Betterway Home books!

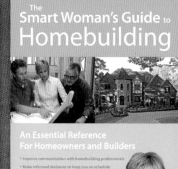
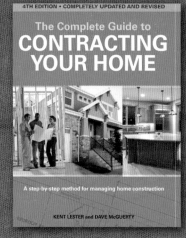
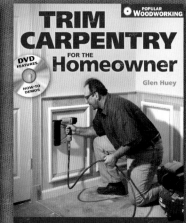